Beginning jQuery

From the Basics of jQuery to Writing your Own Plug-ins

Second Edition

T0225046

Jack Franklin

Russ Ferguson

Apress®

Beginning jQuery: From the Basics of jQuery to Writing your Own Plug-ins

Jack Franklin
London,
United Kingdom

Russ Ferguson
Ocean, New Jersey,
USA

ISBN-13 (pbk): 978-1-4842-3026-8
https://doi.org/10.1007/978-1-4842-3027-5

ISBN-13 (electronic): 978-1-4842-3027-5

Library of Congress Control Number: 2017960290

Cover image designed by Freepik.

Managing Director: Welmoed Spahr
Editorial Director: Todd Green
Acquisitions Editor: Louise Corrigan
Development Editor: James Markham
Technical Reviewer: Massimo Nardone
Coordinating Editor: Nancy Chen
Copy Editor: Bill McManus
Compositor: SPi Global
Indexer: SPi Global
Artist: SPi Global

Distributed to the book trade worldwide by Springer Science+Business Media New York, 233 Spring Street, 6th Floor, New York, NY 10013. Phone 1-800-SPRINGER, fax (201) 348-4505, e-mail orders-ny@springer-sbm.com, or visit www.springeronline.com. Apress Media, LLC is a California LLC and the sole member (owner) is Springer Science + Business Media Finance Inc (SSBM Finance Inc). SSBM Finance Inc is a **Delaware** corporation.

For information on translations, please e-mail rights@apress.com, or visit http://www.apress.com/rights-permissions.

Apress titles may be purchased in bulk for academic, corporate, or promotional use. eBook versions and licenses are also available for most titles. For more information, reference our Print and eBook Bulk Sales web page at http://www.apress.com/bulk-sales.

Any source code or other supplementary material referenced by the authors in this book is available to readers on GitHub via the book's product page, located at www.apress.com/9781484230268. For more detailed information, please visit http://www.apress.com/source-code.

Printed on acid-free paper

Contents

About the Authors

Jack Franklin is a Developer Evangelist at Pusher. He is a keen blogger, developer, and author. He first started creating web sites back in 2005 and has experience in a number of web languages including HTML, CSS, PHP, Ruby, Python, and others, although his main focus is JavaScript. He runs the popular online resource javascriptplayground.com and has released a number of open source jQuery plug-ins online.

Russ Ferguson is a freelance developer and instructor in the New York City area. His interest in computers goes back to Atari Basic, CompuServe, and BBS systems in the mid-1980s. For over 10 years, he has been fortunate to teach at Pratt Institute, where subjects have been as diverse as the student body. Working in New York has given him the opportunity to work with a diverse group of companies whose projects ranged from developing real-time chat/video applications for start-ups to developing and managing content management systems for established media and advertising agencies such as MTV and DC Comics.

About the Technical Reviewer

Massimo Nardone has more than 22 years of experience in security, web/mobile development, cloud, and IT architecture. His true IT passions are security and Android.

He has been programming and teaching how to program with Android, Perl, PHP, Java, VB, Python, C/C++, and MySQL for more than 20 years.

Massimo holds a Master of Science degree in Computing Science from the University of Salerno, Italy. He has worked variously as a project manager, software engineer, research engineer, chief security architect, information security manager, PCI/SCADA auditor, and senior lead IT security/cloud/SCADA architect over many years.

Massimo's technical skills include: security, Android, cloud, Java, MySQL, Drupal, Cobol, Perl, web and mobile development, MongoDB, D3, Joomla, Couchbase, C/C++, WebGL, Python, Pro Rails, Django CMS, Jekyll, and Scratch, among others.

He currently works as Chief Information Security Office (CISO) for Cargotec Oyj. He worked as visiting lecturer and supervisor for exercises at the Networking Laboratory of the Helsinki University of Technology (Aalto University). He holds four international patents (PKI, SIP, SAML, and Proxy areas).

Massimo has reviewed more than 40 IT books for different publishing companies and is the coauthor of *Pro Android Games* (Apress, 2015).

CHAPTER 1

JavaScript You Need to Know

jQuery is a framework that's built on top of JavaScript, not a language in its own right. It is possible to write jQuery with barely any knowledge of JavaScript, but it's not something we would recommend. If you want to be able to confidently write jQuery plug-ins for your site, or alter plug-ins others have written, you need to be familiar with basic JavaScript. That is why this book starts with JavaScript that you need to know. This chapter covers

- JavaScript scripts on a web page
- Variables and objects in JavaScript
- JavaScript functions
- Conditionals
- Looping over arrays and objects
- Debugging JavaScript

If you are familiar with JavaScript, you might feel like skipping this chapter. That's fine, but please consider skimming it first to ensure that you are comfortable with everything covered. Resist the temptation to skip to the jQuery parts—because you will struggle with it. Trust us, in a couple of chapters' time, this preparation will all seem worth it. Many developers we've helped online have dived into jQuery eagerly before quickly becoming stuck due to a lack of understanding the language jQuery is built on. When you're writing jQuery, you're writing JavaScript, but using the jQuery library. We cannot stress how important it is that you make sure you are comfortable with the content covered in this chapter before moving on. We suggest that you try out the code as you read through this chapter. Don't fool yourself into thinking you understand it because you've read it; there is no substitute for typing out the code yourself.

To run the code, we recommend using JS Console (`https://jsconsole.com`), a tool by Remy Sharp that allows you to execute JavaScript and see the results. Some alternatives are JS Bin (`http://jsbin.com`) or JSFiddle (`https://jsfiddle.net`). You can enter the code in the browser and see the results. This is really useful for short lines of code. Figure 1-1 shows an example of JS Console.

Figure 1-1. *The Console tab displays the results of the JavaScript tab using JS bin*

For larger pieces of code, it's best to set up an `index.html` page and include your JavaScript file in there. That would be the way you would really put a site together. The next section explains how to do that. Throughout this chapter, several examples use the `alert()` function to demonstrate the value of a certain variable. This is purely used for demonstration of concepts. In real life, when you need to check the variable, you wouldn't ever use alerts—you'd use a browser's JavaScript console. The reason for using alerts for basic examples in this chapter is that it's much easier to get started with. At this point, there's no need to load up the developer tools, which take time to get accustomed to. Once you progress into more complex code later in the chapter, you will spend time exploring the developer tools.

Using JavaScript on a Web Page

Within a typical HTML file, there are typically two ways to add JavaScript to a page. To add some JavaScript, you can either add your code inline, within a `script` tag, like so:

```
<script type="text/javascript">
  //write code here
</script>
```

Or, you can create an external JavaScript file with the `.js` file extension and then load it in, through the `script` tag:

```
<script type="text/javascript" src="path/to/your/file.js"></script>
```

■ **Note** You have to close the `script` tag.

The first location is within the head element, and the second is just before the closing `</body>` tag. In the past, scripts were always loaded into the head element, but with performance and page loading speeds more critical than ever, it's often recommended to place your scripts at the bottom of your page. This is an approach we side with, too.

The browser renders the page from top to bottom, and when it comes across your scripts, it pauses rendering the page to load in your JS:. Thus, the page loads slower (or, more importantly, feels that way to the user) because the rendering is blocked by your loading JavaScript files. Hence, putting the scripts just before the closing `</body>` tag means that when the time comes to load your scripts, the rest of the page has been loaded.

Before moving on to looking at the language itself, there's one more thing to note. Using the HTML5 doctype (`<!DOCTYPE html>`), you don't actually need to define the type attribute on your script tags. Simply using the following is sufficient:

```
<script src="path/to/your/file.js"></script>
```

This does not cause issues in older browsers—neither does the HTML5 doctype—and we highly recommend using it.

Syntax Conventions

JavaScript's syntax is pretty basic and clear, but there are certain subtleties that you will discover on the way. There's often more than one way to do things, but the community has certain conventions that have stuck over time.

Semicolons

One convention that we want to mention straightaway is the use of semicolons. Often in JavaScript, adding a semicolon at the end of a line is optional, and you will see tutorials that don't do it. However, the convention is to always use a semicolon at the end of a line, and that's what we'll be following in this book. There are obviously certain circumstances when you can't use one, and you will see those in this book, but in any situation where a semicolon is optional, we'll use one. We recommend you do, too.

White Space

Another consideration to make is for white space. It is insignificant in JavaScript, so you can lay out code the way you like in terms of white space. Whenever you are inside a set of braces, you should indent by one tab, but other than that, you will find yourself adapting your own standard.

Comments

Before continuing, at this stage it's worth discussing comments. JavaScript allows you to insert comments in your code. This is content that will be ignored and not treated as code, so you can put anything you want in comments. Inserting comments is useful for documenting your code. There are two syntaxes for comments—one for a single-line comment and one for a multiline comment:

```
//this is a single-line comment, denoted by two forward slashes
/* this is a multiline comment, started with a slash and an asterisk
and ended with an asterisk and a slash */
```

Use comments to remind yourself about a piece of code and what it does, or to provide references for the future you. After not working on code for a long period of time, comments can really help you remember why you wrote what you wrote.

Variables

Often when coding, you want to save the state of something. Perhaps you want to remember that the current color of your background is red, or the calculation you just performed totaled 33. JavaScript, like most languages, has *variables*: a place to store information. To create a variable, you simply declare it with the var keyword, name it, and then set it to equal to something. You can also declare a variable without explicitly setting its value. If you do this, the variable will be set to undefined, a special value in JavaScript that simply means that this variable has not been set to anything. The following examples declare three variables:

```
var twoPlusThree = 5;
var twoPlusTwo = 2 + 2;
var notYetDefined;
```

The first variable, twoPlusThree, is set to the value 5. The second, twoPlusTwo, is set to be the result of 2+2. Here you meet one of JavaScript's many operators, +. These operators perform operations on values. Most of them are obvious. Along with + (addition), there's – (subtraction), / (division), * (multiplication), and many more. You'll meet more throughout the book, so don't worry too much about them now. The third variable, notYetDefined, does not have a value and is set to undefined, because we declared a variable (that is, we created a new variable) but did not set a value.

Creating Variables

Variables can contain letters, digits, and underscores. They cannot start with a number. So the variable name 0abc is *not* valid, whereas abc0 is. Typically, most developers do not use digits in variable names, and either stick to camelCase or the underscore notation.

■ **Note** Notice our naming convention for variables. We're using what's known as camelCase, which means the first word in the variable name should start with a lowercase letter but then every other word in the name should start with a capital letter. We'll be using this convention throughout the book. There are other popular naming conventions, most notably the_underscore_method. This keeps all words in lowercase and separates them with underscores. This is more popular in other languages. The majority of the JavaScript community uses camelCase.

Of course, once you set a variable to a value, it doesn't mean you can't change the value. All variables can have their values changed. You do it very similarly to the way you declare a variable, with the only difference being the missing var keyword at the beginning. That's only needed when you declare a variable. This example sets the totalCost to 5, and then updates it again to be 5 + 3 (which you could just write as 8, obviously):

```
var totalCost = 5;
totalCost = 5 + 3;
```

Types

Before continuing, you will notice that so far all the variables have been set as nondecimal numbers. In JavaScript (and all programming languages), there is the notion of types. A variable can be any of several types. The most common are the number type and the string type. There's also the Boolean type, which can only be set to true or false. When working with JavaScript, you usually won't have to worry too much about types. Even if a variable is declared with an integer value (e.g., 5), you can update it to be a string value, as follows:

```
var testVariable = 5;
testVariable = "Jack";
```

This changes the type of testVariable from an integer to a string, and JavaScript doesn't complain at all. Along with strings, numbers, and Booleans, the two other types you need to concern yourself with (for now) are arrays and objects. Both are covered in more detail very shortly, but for now, just know that an *array* is essentially a list of values. These values can be of any type, and not all values within an array have to be the same type. You can create an array by listing values between square braces, like so:

```
var squares = [1, 4, 9, 16, 25];
```

```
var mixed = [1, "Jack", 5, true, 6.5, "Franklin"];
```

For now, that's all you need to know about arrays.

The other type, object, is more easily explained with an example. Let's say you have the concept of a car in your application. This car has a certain number of wheels and seats, is a certain color, and has a maximum speed. You could model this car with four separate variables:

```
var carWheelCount = 4;
var carColor = "red";
```

```
var carSeatCount = 5;
var carMaximumSpeed = 99;
```

It would be easier if you could have just one variable—car—that contained all this information. This is what an object does. It's a way to store lots of information (that is usually related) within one variable. If you were using objects, the previous code for the car might look something like this:

```
var car = {
  wheelCount: 4,
  color: "red",
  seatCount: 5,
  carMaximumSpeed: 99
};
```

The syntax for creating an object is a little different from anything else you've seen so far, so let's walk through it. You create the variable as normal, but then to create an object, you wrap it in curly braces. An object is a set of key-value pairs, also referred to as *properties*. You create these by listing them in the format key: value, putting a comma at the end of all but the last property. This is a much nicer way to model your code programmatically.

To access properties within the object, you have two choices:

```
car.wheelCount;
car["wheelCount"];
```

The reason for having two ways of accessing properties is easily demonstrated. The vast majority of the time, you will be using the first version, the dot notation. The only time you'll need to use the second version is if you need to access a key in an object when the name of that key is stored in a variable. This is clearer to see in a demonstration. Let's say that the key you want to access, wheelCount, is stored in a variable due to some prior code in your application. If you want to get at the value at wheelCount, you have to use the second notation, as follows:

```
var keyToGet = "wheelCount";
car[keyToGet]; //this will give us 4
```

This situation doesn't happen a lot, but sometimes you need to use it. You will see examples of this much later in the book. For now, let's move on.

Functions

Once you've written some code that you might want to use again elsewhere, you have two options. You could simply copy the code again when you need to use it—but that's not a good approach. If you need to change it, you'd have to change it in two or more places. It would be better to create a function.

Creating Functions

This lets you reuse code in multiple places, and if you need to make a change, you only have to change it in one place. Creating a function is very straightforward. Use the function keyword to denote that you are creating a new function. You then name it and place the code for your function within curly braces.

```
function alertTwo() {
  alert("2");
}
```

All this function does is show an alert displaying "2" on your screen. Note that the brackets (or parentheses) after the function name are empty. This means that the function you've declared doesn't take any arguments. You might declare another function that takes an argument and alerts it, like in the following:

```
function alertSomething(something) {
  alert(something);
}
```

This function is passed in an argument, which within the function is a variable you can refer to as something. All you do is alert the value of that variable, as follows:

```
alertSomething("Jack");
alertSomething(2);
```

If you were to run this code in a browser, two alert boxes would pop up, the first showing the text "Jack". Once you clicked the alert box to dismiss it, another box containing the number "2" would pop up.

Functions can take multiple arguments, too, such as:

```
function alertThings(thing1, thing2) {
  alert(thing1);
  alert(thing2);
}

alertThings("Jack", "Franklin");
```

As in the prior example, this also gives you two alerts. The first containing "Jack" and the second "Franklin".

Something that's done very often in jQuery development is to pass in an object to a function rather than multiple variables. Calling a function and passing in multiple arguments can get confusing; for example:

```
someFunction("Jack", "Franklin", 1, 2, 3, 4, "a", "x");
```

So a lot of plug-ins—something jQuery makes use of extensively—pass in an object to a function. For example, if you're declaring a function that takes three to four or more arguments, you'd probably let the function take in an object, as follows:

```
function aPerson(person) {
  alert(person.firstName);
  alert(person.lastName);
  alert(person.age);
}

var jack = {
  firstName: "Jack",
  lastName: "Franklin",
  age: 20
}

aPerson(jack);
```

If you run that code, you will see three alerts, each alerting the properties of the object stored in the jack variable. This is a pattern used when working extensively with jQuery, so make sure you understand what's going on here. To avoid passing in a large number of arguments to a function—which makes it tough to remember which argument is which and the order they go in—developers will often write their functions to accept an object as the only argument. This means each argument can be named—the order doesn't matter—and as a developer, it's much easier to look over the code and see what's going on.

Rather than cover functions and all their details now, they will be discussed in context in subsequent chapters. Before moving on, however, you need to understand the concept of functions returning values.

Functions Returning Values

Functions are often used as a way of performing some calculation, such as converting inches to centimeters. This is a function that you expect to pass in a value, and for it to compute and "return" a value. The following examples shows how you would do this:

```
function inchesToCM(inches) {
  return inches * 2.54;
}

var sixFeetInInches = 72;
var sixFeetInCM = inchesToCM(sixFeetInInches);
```

This leaves sixFeetInCM as 182.88, which is 72 multiplied by 2.54. The reason the sixFeetInCM variable is given that value is because the inchesToCM() function is returning its argument—inches—multiplied by 2.54. By returning the argument, the sixFeetInCM variable is set to whatever inches * 2.54 gives you.

Functions can return absolutely any value. Often you might want to return a Boolean, either true or false, as follows:

```
function isItSunnyInBritain() {
  return false;
}

var isSunny = isItSunnyInBritain();
```

This function will return false, as it should. Let's face it, it's never sunny in Britain! Returning values from functions is something that you'll use frequently.

Conditionals

Something you'll often want to do is run code conditionally. That is, only do something if something else is true or false. For example, alert "child" if the age variable is less than 12. JavaScript has this ability through if statements:

```
var age = 10;
if(age < 12) {
  alert("Child");
}
```

But what if you wanted to do something else if the age is greater than 12? Along with the if statement, you can attach an else onto the end of that, as follows:

```
var age = 15;
if(age < 12) {
  alert("Child");
} else {
  alert("Not a child");
}
```

Here you've met another operator—the less-than symbol, <. There's also its opposite, greater than, >, as well as "less than or equal to" and "greater than or equal to," <= and >=, respectively. If you want to check multiple conditions, you can also use else if, like so:

```
if(age <= 12) {
  alert("Child");
} else if (age < 20) {
  alert("Teenager");
} else {
  alert("Adult");
}
```

Of course, you can use multiple else if statements if required, but usually you won't need more than one or perhaps two. Anything that can be evaluated to true or false can be used as the condition of an if statement. An easier way to get your head around this is to imagine putting some statement within those brackets and in your mind calculating whether this statement is true or false. If you are able to do that, your condition can be used within an if statement.

```
var name = "Jack";
var age = 20;

if(age > 18 && name === "Jack") {
  alert("Hello Jack, you're older than 18!");
}
```

There's two new things to discuss here. First, you have combined two conditionals into one with the "and" operator, &&. This means the condition will only evaluate to true if both the left and right sides of that condition evaluate to true.

Second, you've just seen how to check equality. In JavaScript, this is a complicated area. You can use both == and === to check equality, with both having subtle but important differences. For now, trust us when we tell you to *always* use ===.

Along with &&, there's also ||, which is the "or" operator. Let's see this in action:

```
var age = 19;
var name = "bob"; if(age > 18 || name === "Jack") {
  alert("your name is Jack or you're older than 18");
}
```

The alert will still be shown here, even though only one of the conditional statements holds true. Age is indeed greater than 18, which makes it irrelevant that the name of this person isn't Jack, because the or operator will return true as long as one of the conditions is met.

Make sure you understand the difference between || and &&. The first evaluates to true if *either* of the conditions evaluates to true; whereas && evaluates to true if *both* the conditions evaluate to true.

It's also possible to *negate* conditionals, meaning they pass if the reverse is true, as follows:

```
var age = 20;
if(!age < 18) {
  alert("Hello adult");
}
```

The negation operator, !, reverses the outcome of the conditional. In this example, age < 18 is false, but the ! that prefixes the conditional reverses false to true.

In general, you should try to avoid negations like the preceding one, writing it as age >= 18 rather than !age < 18, because it makes the code easier to read. The quicker one can scan the code and assess its function, the better.

Debugging with the Console

Earlier, we briefly mentioned the developer console available in browsers. We stated that once we got to more complex examples, we'd switch from using alert() to using console.log(). Before making that switch, you need to take a look at the debugging available to you.

Modern browsers ship with a JavaScript console, which is an invaluable tool in the JavaScript developer's arsenal. The following list describes how you access the console in all modern browsers:

- **IE10+:** Press F12 and click the Console tab.

- **Chrome:** Alt+Cmd+J on macOS. Ctrl+Shift+J on Windows.

- **Safari:** Alt+Cmd+I on macOS. Ctrl+Alt+I on Windows.

- **Firefox:** Alt+Cmd+K on macOS. Ctrl+Shift+K on Windows.

- **Opera:** Alt+Cmd+I on macOS. Ctrl+Shift+I on Windows.

I use Google Chrome as my browser of choice, all screenshots in this book are from Chrome's console (unless ortherwisde noted) but all browsers have a very similar feature set and they look the same, so pick the one that suits you best. Look at the example in Figure 1-2.

```
⊗  🔲 Elements  📄 Resources  ● Network  📝 Sources  🕑 Timeline  🔲 Profiles  🔲 Audits  📝 Console
> var x = 2;
  undefined
> x
  2
> |
```

Figure 1-2. After declaring a variable, viewing its value in Google Chrome's JS console

9

The console is great for trying out pieces of code, but it really shines for debugging. The most popular method is `console.log()`, which will log data to the console for you to see. From now on in this chapter, the examples use this method as opposed to `alert()`. When working with complex data structures, `console.log()` provides a much nicer way to view the values of variables.

To see an example, create the following HTML file—name it something sensible—and then open it in a browser with developer tools:

```html
<!DOCTYPE html>
<html>
  <head>
    <title>Hey</title>
    <script type="text/javascript" charset="utf-8">
      console.log("Jack");
    </script>
  </head>
  <body>
  </body>
</html>
```

If you bring up the developer console by following the previous instructions, you should see something like Figure 1-3.

Figure 1-3. *The string "Jack" being logged to the console*

You can log absolutely anything to the console and it will know how to deal with it. You'll see this in action now as you dive into arrays.

Arrays

Before moving on to jQuery, it's important to cover arrays. An array is simply a list of values, as mentioned earlier. The following is an example of an array:

```javascript
var classMates = ["Jack", "Jamie", "Rich", "Will"];
```

That's about as much as covered earlier, so now it's time to delve further.

You can access a single element in an array by adding a number in square brackets after the variable, like so:

```javascript
classMates[1]; //Jamie
```

Notice here that the element at position 1 is not "Jack", but "Jamie". This is because arrays are *zero-indexed*. That is, the first element in an array is actually at position 0, not position 1. This can take some time to get used to if you're not a programmer, but once you get the hang of it, it will become second nature. So to get the name "Jack" from the array, you would need to use classMates[0]. You can find out the length of an array by using classMates.length, which in this case returns 4. As a quick test, how do you think you might get at the last element of an array when you don't know the length?

You'd do it like so:

```
classMates[classMates.length - 1]; // "Will"
```

See if you can figure out how this works without reading the explanation first. classMates.length gives the array length, which is 4. So to get the last item in the array, you need to get the person at the last index, which is the length minus one, down to the fact that the first element is at position 0 and not position 1.

Remember, JavaScript arrays can contain absolutely anything within them, including objects and also other arrays. Here's what you might call a *two-dimensional array*, an array in which each element is itself an array:

```
var twoDArray = [
  ["Jack", "Jon", "Fred"],
  ["Sue", "Heather", "Amy"]
];
```

To access elements in an array of arrays, use the square bracket notation, just as you used it previously, to get the second element in the classMates array, classMates[1]:

```
twoDArray[0][0]; //Jack
twoDArray[1][0]; //Sue
twoDArray[1][2]; //Amy
```

The first set of square brackets grabs the element of twoDArray, so twoDArray[0] returns the array containing "Jack", "Jon", and "Fred". twoDArray[1] is the array containing "Sue", "Heather", and "Amy".

This isn't something you'll have to do very often, but it's worth showing you in this introduction to JavaScript because it really makes certain that you understand the basics of arrays.

To add an element to an array, use the push() method:

```
classMates.push("Catherine");
```

Note that push() will always add an element to the end of an array.

Unfortunately, there's no such method for easily removing items in arrays. You can use the delete operator, which at first glance does everything you need:

```
delete classMates[1]
```

While this looks like it will work, it actually doesn't. If you perform that command on your initial array of "Jack", "Jamie", "Rich", "Will", this is what happens:

```
delete classMates[1];
console.log(classMates); //["Jack", undefined, "Rich", "Will"]
```

This is the crucial aspect of delete: it does not remove the element from the array. It simply replaces the value at that index with undefined. Hence, to actually completely remove an element from an array, you have some more work to do. You will revisit this later in the book when this problem actually occurs.

Loops

Now that you know the basics of using arrays, you are ready to learn about looping. It's only natural that once you have a list of items, you often want to go through each item in turn and perform some calculation or function on it. The two loops you'll meet here are the while loop and the for loop.

The while loop is very simple and actually takes on the form of something you've already seen, the if statement. The basic while loop looks something like this:

```
while(condition) {
        //code
}
```

The code within the braces will execute continually while the condition evaluates to true. This has a number of use cases, but most frequently it's used to iterate over a list, which is done like so:

```
var count = 0;
while(count < classMates.length) {
  alert(classMates[count]);
  count++;
}
```

If you were to run that code, you'd get five alerts—"Jack", "Jamie", and so on—for each of the five items in the classMates array (in a prior example, you used the push() method to add a fifth, "Catherine"). Taking this line by line, here's how it works:

- First, you set a new count variable equal to 0.

- Your condition for the code to execute is that the count variable must be less than the length of classMates.length.

- If it is, you do two things:

    - First, alert the value at classMates[count], which will be classMates[0], then classMates[1], up to classMates[3]—the last time the count variable is less than the length of classMates.

    - Second, run count++, which is a new operator you've not seen. It's simply a shortcut for count = count + 1, so it increments the count variable by 1.

You will find yourself using the while loop very often. Of course, it doesn't have to be used with arrays—you can use it without, but it will cause an infinite loop, so we wouldn't recommend running it. Here's an example:

```
while(1 < 5) {
  alert("hello");
}
```

Here the condition, 1 < 5, will always be true, so the code inside the loop will be executed over and over again. Most modern browsers will detect this and prevent the code from crashing the browser, but even so, we wouldn't recommend running it.

Along with the while loop, there's also a for loop. The syntax for this is slightly different:

```
for(before loop; condition; iteration) {
        //code
}
```

Within the arguments for a for loop, you define three things:

- The code to be run *before* the loop starts

- The condition that must be met so that the code within the braces can execute

- The code that is run at the end of *every* iteration

This is best illustrated with an example. The following will display the numbers 0 through 9:

```
for(var i = 0; i < 10; i++) {
  alert(i);
}
```

If you wanted to loop through the classMates array using a for loop instead of a while, it's done like so:

```
for(var i = 0; i < classMates.length; i++) {
  alert(classMates[i]);
}
```

Compare this to the while loop:

```
var count = 0;
while(count < classMates.length) {
  alert(classMates[count]);
  count++;
}
```

The only differences are that the initial var count = 0; has moved to within the parentheses of the for, and count++ is moved to the end of the parentheses. Often developers will use count as the variable to loop over some code; other times, you'll see i used, as in "iterator." Of course, you can use any variable name you like, but those two tend to be the most popular. We'll use i for most of this book, but if you prefer the more verbose count, or anything similar, feel free to use it.

With a while loop or a for loop, you can edit the values of the array when you loop over them, as follows:

```
var i = 0;
while(i < classMates.length) {
  classMates [i] = "Class Mate " + i;
  i++;
}
```

That would update your classMates array to be

```
["Class Mate 0", "Class Mate 1", "Class Mate 2", "Class Mate 3"]
```

Before this chapter ends, there's one more thing about a for loop that you need to know. When working with an object, you can use the combination of a for loop with the in operator to loop over the properties:

```
var classMates = {
  "Jamie" : 20,
  "Will": 21,
  "Rich": 22,
  "Jack": 23
}

for(classMate in classMates) {
  console.log(classMate + " is " + classMates[classMate] + " years old");
}
```

This will give you the following output:

```
Jamie is 20 years old

Will is 21 years old

Rich is 22 years old

Jack is 23 years old
```

The key here is the first line, for(classMate in classMates) {}. This loops over the classMates object and loops over every property in the object. You can then get at the value at that property through classMates[classMate].

More console.log()

You used console.log() when looking at arrays, but you've so far only used it in the most basic form by passing it one argument that you expect it to log to the console. It's much more powerful than that. You can pass in multiple arguments and it will log them all out—on the same line. For example:

```
var classMates = ["Jack", "Jamie", "Rich", "Will"];
var twoPlusTwo = 4;
console.log(classMates);
console.log("twoPlusTwo", twoPlusTwo);
```

You will see the output shown in Figure 1-4.

Figure 1-4. *The console logging out your array and variable*

You can see that logging out the `classMates` array makes it completely clear what it contains, and this is exactly what `console.log()` is there for. If you want to output more than one thing on one line, you can easily do that by passing in multiple arguments to the function. The second example logs out the string `"twoPlusTwo"` and then the variable `twoPlusTwo`. We often do this when logging a lot of values, so it's clearer in the console which line is logging what. We will be using `console.log()` heavily throughout this book.

Summary

This chapter covered a lot of JavaScript basics, including variables, `if` statements, loops, arrays, objects, and a lot more, and now you have a solid grounding. As you move into jQuery, we'll regularly stop along the way to make sure that you're comfortable with the JavaScript behind what you're doing. Strap yourself in, because in the next chapter, it's time to move on and meet jQuery.

CHAPTER 2

■ ■ ■

The Basics of jQuery

jQuery is a powerful and complex library that was first released in August 2006, although the initial idea came much earlier. Before diving in, there's time for a very brief history lesson on how the library came to be.

The first time anything posted online that hinted that a potential library was forming was on August 22, 2005. jQuery's founder, John Resig, posted a blog post titled "Selectors in JavaScript" (`https://johnresig.com/blog/selectors-in-javascript/`), which demonstrated Resig's idea that we could interact with elements in JavaScript using CSS selectors. This demonstrated a new idea that would eventually form the beginnings of the library we know and love today. jQuery was officially announced at Bar Camp NYC in January 2006 and it quickly took the Internet by storm, topping the front pages of many popular sites. jQuery grew and grew, and hit stable v1 in August 2006. From there it has continued to grow. Its impact on web development cannot be underestimated, and its impact on the community view of JavaScript is even more important.

In this chapter, you will do the following:

- Look at how browsers represent web pages through the Document Object Model (DOM).

- Look at DOM nodes and the terms *parent*, *child*, and *sibling* in the context of a web page.

- Download the jQuery source and include it in a web page.

- Write some code that utilizes jQuery.

- Explore in detail how that code works, and meet some of jQuery's features.

- Explore the jQuery API documentation and how to use it to answer any issues you might have.

jQuery made JavaScript more accessible to the "average" developer. For example, which of the following two syntaxes do you prefer for selecting an element by its ID?

```
document.getElementById("example");
```

or

```
$("#example");
```

Suddenly, if you knew how to select elements with CSS, you could transfer that knowledge to JavaScript by using jQuery. jQuery provided a reliable cross-browser method of interacting with the Document Object Model. Before we get much further, it's time to discuss the DOM.

© Jack Franklin, Russ Ferguson 2017
J. Franklin, R. Ferguson, *Beginning jQuery*, https://doi.org/10.1007/978-1-4842-3027-5_2

The Document Object Model (DOM)

When you look at a web site, you see a lot of elements grouped together and styled to form what's in front of you. To be able to access those elements through code to remove, add, and manipulate them, you need some form of *interface*—a representation of the elements on a page that is structured and follows a set of rules on how to model them. This is what the DOM is. The DOM also lets you capture browser events—such as a user clicking a link, submitting a form, or scrolling down the page. In Chapter 3 you will see how to use jQuery to traverse the DOM.

In the early days of the Web and browsers, standards in terms of JavaScript implementation were not very clear. This led to browsers implementing features in different ways, which caused developers issues. It led to any JavaScript having to effectively be written multiple times for the different browsers that had different implementations—primarily Netscape and Internet Explorer (IE).

Thankfully, as things progressed, browsers adopted the same standards and things settled down. However, the level at which browsers support the DOM can still cause issues today. In particular, we're not free of the older versions of Internet Explorer, which do not support the DOM to the level of more-modern browsers. This is one reason jQuery is so valuable: everything it offers works just as well in an older version of IE as it does in the latest release of Google Chrome or Mozilla Firefox. It is important to note that the last version of IE is 11; Microsoft Edge is now the default browser in Windows 10.

Before continuing with jQuery (you'll get there soon!), it's worth taking a moment to introduce how the DOM works. When a page is loaded, the browser generates a representation of what's on the page, and for each element, it generates one or more *nodes* that represent it. There are multiple types of nodes, and were this a book purely on DOM interaction with JavaScript, we'd be covering the DOM in more detail.

As we mentioned in the first chapter, we feel it's very important to give people new to jQuery a solid introduction to the foundations on which jQuery is built. We've already covered JavaScript in great detail, and we feel it's important to look at the DOM. When a browser forms a representation of the current page as the DOM, every element is a node. Let's say you have a paragraph with some text in it, such as:

```
<p>Hello World</p>
```

That's not one node, but two nodes. There's a *text node* that contains "Hello World" and an *element node* that's the paragraph.

■ **Note**   The text node would be a *child* of the element node because it resides within it. In a typical page, there are a lot of nested nodes.

A `div` with two paragraphs that both have text within them is structured like so:

```
div element node
-- paragraph element node
---- text node
-- paragraph element node
---- text node
```

The two paragraphs in this instance are *siblings* because they have the same *parent node*. The paragraphs are *children* of the `div`, but the text nodes are not child nodes because they are not direct descendants of the `div` element. They are child nodes of the paragraph nodes. There are three main types of nodes that you need to know: element, text, and attribute nodes. Let's say that you gave the paragraph a class, such as:

```
<p class="intro">Hello World</p>
```

There are now three nodes at play:

- The *element node* representing your paragraph

- A *text node* that contains the text "Hello World"

- An *attribute node* that states this element has class="intro"

Somewhat confusingly, an attribute node is *not* considered to be a child of an element node.

Between those elements, they make up the vast majority of most of the web pages out there. Before (finally) getting to jQuery, make certain that you understand the following terms because they are used continually throughout the book:

- *child node*: A node that is a direct descendant of another node, usually an element node

- *parent node*: A node that has direct descendants (e.g., children)

- *siblings*: Two nodes that share the same parent

And just to iterate one final time, the following is a visual representation:

```
div parent
-- p child of div, sibling of p
---- "hello world" - child of p
-- p child of div, sibling of p
---- strong child of p
------ "hello" child of strong
```

Understanding the terms "child," "parent," and "siblings" will be very important later in the book when we discuss selecting elements with jQuery, so make sure you're confident about their meanings.

Downloading jQuery

After a lot of preparation, you are ready to dive into jQuery and use it for the first time. The best place to start is the jQuery web site at http://jquery.com (see Figure 2-1).

Figure 2-1. *The jQuery home page*

Click the large Download jQuery button (or the Download tab) on the jQuery home page to open to the Download page. Here you are given instructions on the many ways you can add jQuery to a project. For example, if you want to add jQuery locally, you can download either the compressed version or the uncompressed version. If you are using npm (Node Package Manager) or Bower (another package manager), you can find the instructions here. In addition, there are instructions for using a CDN (content delivery network) and for a few other ways.

If you click the "Download jQuery" button on the home page. You are presented with multiple options to download jQuery. There are two compression-level options listed on the download page:

- Production (87KB), Minified and Gzipped

- Development (268KB), Uncompressed Code

Unless you want to study the jQuery source in detail for every project that you create using jQuery, always pick the Production version. This code has been run through a *minifier*, a program that compresses JavaScript files into smaller versions. Minifiers perform a number of actions to get the code down to as small as possible, including

- Stripping out all white space.

- Removing all comments.

- Renaming long variable names; for example, `var myCar` might become `var a`.

Minified code is completely unreadable, but it's not designed to be readable—it's designed to make the file as small as possible. From now on when we refer to the *jQuery source*, we're referring to the minified version of jQuery.

Some developers link to a CDN-hosted version of jQuery, the most popular of which is Google's CDN (`https://developers.google.com/speed/libraries/#jquery`). These allow you to include jQuery by referencing the jQuery file that's hosted on their CDN. If you wanted to include the latest version of jQuery from Google's CDN, you'd do it like so:

```
<script src="http://ajax.googleapis.com/ajax/libs/jquery/3.2.1/jquery.min.js"></script>
```

Doing it this way brings advantages. If the user has visited another site that references jQuery in this way, they may have the file cached already, meaning the browser does not have to download it again. For examples in this book, however, we've chosen to download a version of jQuery locally for one simple reason: you don't need the Internet to work through the examples. It may sound foolish, but more than once, one of our authors has been ready to do some work while on a train, only to remember he referenced the Google CDN version of jQuery, and he didn't have an Internet connection.

The jQuery API Documentation

If you are using jQuery, you need a good source from which to learn what each API does. The jQuery documentation (`http://api.jquery.com`) lists every method jQuery provides. Another reason jQuery has become so successful is its documentation, which is *fantastic*. We seriously cannot overstate how good we think the documentation is (see Figure 2-2).

Figure 2-2. *The jQuery API index page*

There are a couple of ways to find what you're looking for on the web site. If you know exactly which method you want, using the search box located at the top right of the screen is by far the quickest way. If you're not certain about exactly what you want—perhaps you're looking for a method to do something particular, but you're not sure if it exists—you can browse the jQuery API categories listed on the left side of the screen to narrow your search. You don't need to look at these yet, but you will return to the API many times. Put it on your bookmarks bar, or find an easy way to browse it, as you will use it a lot.

Writing Some jQuery

Save your downloaded jQuery file as `jquery.js` in a new folder on your machine. You're also going to add an HTML file to this folder, so create an `index.html` page, too. Finally, you want to write all the JavaScript in an individual file, so create `app.js`. This code is available within `02/code/ex1`.

Load the HTML page in your editor of choice—I personally use Vim we highly recommend Sublime Text 2 (`www.sublimetext.com/2`), Visual Studio Code (`https://code.visualstudio.com`), or Atom (`https://atom.io`), all of which run on Windows, macOS, and Linux—and add the following:

```
<!DOCTYPE html>
<html>
  <head>
    <title>Chapter 02, Exercise 01</title>
    <script src="jquery.js"></script>
    <script src="app.js"></script>
  </head>
  <body>
    <p>Hello World</p>
  </body>
</html>
```

This is just a basic HTML page, nothing fancy. Take a look at the two `<script>` tags

```
<script src="jquery.js"></script>
<script src="app.js"></script>
```

First, load in jQuery and then load in the `app.js` file, which is currently blank.

■ **Note** The order of the files being loaded with the `script` tag is very important. Remember that the code you write is going to be dependent on jQuery, so you have to load jQuery before any scripts that use it.

Now that you have your page, go ahead and load `index.html` in your browser. You won't see anything yet, other than the "Hello World" text. Go into `app.js` and add the following line—the first line of jQuery you've written in the book!

```
$("body").css("background", "red");
```

Can you guess what that does? You have already seen that `$("body")` selects the "body" tag (remember, they are just CSS selectors), and you can probably take a logical stab at what `css("background", "red")` does. Refresh the page, and you … won't see any change.

This is a mistake that many jQuery beginners make when starting out. The problem is back in your `index.html` file:

```html
<!DOCTYPE html>
<html>
  <head>
    <meta charset='utf-8' />
    <title>Chapter 02, Exercise 01</title>
    <script src="jquery.js"></script>
    <script src="app.js"></script>
  </head>
  <body>
    <p>Hello World</p>
  </body>
</html>
```

Load in your JavaScript *before* you load in the rest of the page, so when your JavaScript is executed, the page hasn't fully loaded, which means the *DOM is not ready*. Because the page isn't fully loaded at the time your JavaScript is run, the browser hasn't completed constructing the DOM, which means as far as the DOM is concerned, "body" doesn't exist when your JavaScript runs. You have two options here:

- Include your JavaScript at the bottom of the page, just before the closing `</body>`. This means it's run after the DOM is loaded.

- Tell your JavaScript not to execute until the DOM is ready.

In practice, it's better to include JavaScript at the bottom so that it doesn't delay the content loading. So for most of this book, we'll be doing that. This time, however, we're going to choose the second option—purely because we need to explain how you go about doing it. In order to discuss how to stop your code from running until the DOM has loaded, we are going to talk briefly about events. We will cover events in vast detail in Chapter 4, but you need to dip your toes in the topic now.

Within the browser, writing JavaScript is very much *event based*. Write code that's executed based on an event. The user clicks a button, scrolls down the page, hovers over an image, and so on. Each of these actions causes an event to fire, which is grabbed by JavaScript, and then the code is executed based on that event occurring.

The browser also emits an event *when the DOM is loaded*. You can then write code that is only executed *when that event fires*, meaning you know your code will only be executed when the DOM is all set and ready to rock. With jQuery, you do it like so:

```
$(function() {
  //DOM is ready to go
});
```

Let's break down this line:

$(document): This passes the document variable into jQuery. The document variable is a special variable that contains references to all the HTML elements on the page. When this object fires a ready event, you want to execute some code.

.ready(): ready is one of the many events jQuery supports. You pass into it a function that is executed when the ready event is fired. Because you're doing $(document).ready(), the function you pass in is fired when a ready event is registered on the document object.

function() {}: What you pass into the ready call is a regular JavaScript function, which will then be called when the event is emitted. This is like creating functions, as you did in Chapter 1, but instead of naming them, you just pass one straight in. You could do it like so:

```
function onReady() {
  alert("READY TO GO!");
}
$(document).ready(onReady);
```

But in practice, it's easier just to create the function and pass it immediately into the event handler without explicitly naming it first. By doing this, you create an *anonymous function*, a function that doesn't have a name.

The preceding line represents all of the following:

```
$(function() {
  $("body").css("background", "red");
});
```

When you refresh index.html, you'll see a red background! Now, doing $(document).ready(function() {}) is so common, jQuery has a handy shortcut. You can simply do the following:

```
$(function() {
});
```

And that means *exactly the same thing.* If jQuery detects you've passed it a function, it will presume that function should be executed on the DOM already. It's a handy little shortcut to save you a small amount of typing.

The phrase "jQuery detects you've passed it a function" in the preceding paragraph means that when you're selecting something like $("body");, what you're actually doing is calling a function that jQuery provides, which is stored as a variable called the $ symbol. You could easily do this, too. The following code is valid because JavaScript doesn't mind variables having the $ symbol in them or variable names being just one character long:

```
var $ = function() { console.log("hey"); };
$(); //logs "hey" to the console
```

■ **Note**   Don't do the preceding if you've got jQuery on the page, because you'll overwrite the $ variable—meaning it won't reference jQuery anymore.

So all jQuery does is have a function bound to $, which is clever. It can detect what you pass into it, and do certain things. So when you pass in $("body");, it knows to select the body element. But when you pass in $(function() {});, it detects you passed in a function, and acts accordingly.

Now, try something a bit more complicated. In the <head> of your HTML page, add a link to a new style sheet, which you should also create, as follows:

```
<link rel="stylesheet" type="text/css" href="style.css" />
```

Get rid of your Hello World paragraph, and replace it with the following HTML within the <body> tag:

```
<div id="box">my box</div>
```

Head into style.css and add the following:

```
#box {
  width: 100px;
  height: 100px;
  text-align: center;
  background: #f00;
  font-size: 14px;
}
```

Finally, edit your app.js to be simply:

```
$(function() {
});
```

You should see a simple screen like the one shown in Figure 2-3.

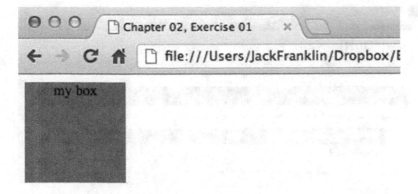

Figure 2-3. *The resulting box*

It's not going to win any design awards, but now you can do some fun stuff with this box. First, create a variable that will store a reference to the div with the ID "box", as follows:

```
var box = $("#box");
```

Save the reference to it as a variable because you're going to use it more than once. Doing the following is inefficient because you're making jQuery select the element twice every time you use $("#box"):

```
$("#box").doSomething();
$("#box").doSomethingElse();
```

It is much better to do it once and save it to a variable.

Animation Example

Now let's look at a jQuery animation example. While animation might seem a daunting prospect, particularly to start with, it's one of the areas that really shows off jQuery's power and gives immediate results, which makes it a good place to start. This example won't go into too much detail, just skim over a few of jQuery's key features. You'll look at each of the areas in great detail later. This is purely a relaxed introduction to jQuery's capabilities.

The first thing you're going to do is fade your box out. Make your app.js file look as follows:

```
$(function() {
  var box = $("#box");
  box.fadeOut("slow");
});
```

Refresh your page—and that lovely red box will slowly fade out of view. It's probably easy to see why the fadeOut() method is aptly named. As you can see, passing in the argument "slow" makes the box fade out slower. You can also use the keywords "normal" and "fast", which do exactly what you'd imagine.

If you want a page that gives you a comprehensive overview of how the fadeOut method works and how to use it, look to the jQuery API documentation. If you search for **fadeOut** and make your way to the documentation for the method, you'll see something like what's shown in Figure 2-4.

Figure 2-4. *The jQuery documentation for the fadeOut() method*

The first bit of the documentation is as follows:

```
.fadeOut( [duration] [, complete] )
duration A string or number determining how long the animation will run.
complete A function to call once the animation is complete.
```

Being able to read and make sense of the API will save you a lot of time. The preceding syntax may be alien right now, but once you know how it works, it's easy to follow because it's consistent throughout the API. The first line describes how the method can be called. This shows that you can call fadeOut() by passing in a duration and a completion function. The square brackets around each argument means the argument is *optional*—you don't have to pass either in. You can pass one argument in, pass both in, or none, and jQuery knows how to handle that. Earlier, you called it as follows:

```
$("#box").fadeOut("slow");
```

You can see that you passed in the duration, but not a completion method. *Callback* is a term used often in JavaScript that refers to a function that is called once something has finished executing. In the context of fadeOut(), this completion function will be called after your box has faded out. To see this in action, change your app.js to the following:

```
$(function() {
  var box = $("#box");
  box.fadeOut("slow", function() {
    alert("box finished fading out");
  });
});
```

Once the box is faded out, you will see an alert on your screen. This gives you great power to be able to do something, and then run something else the moment that original thing is finished. Callbacks are used extensively in jQuery. A vast number of methods, especially animation ones, take callbacks, and you will use them frequently. Of course, because both parameters are optional, you can also pass in just a callback, like so:

```
$(function() {
  var box = $("#box");
  box.fadeOut(function() {
    alert("box finished fading out");
  });
});
```

You'll notice this time when you refresh, the box fades out more quickly. Previously, you were passing in a "slow" speed. But what happens when you don't pass in one? What does jQuery do?

Any argument that is optional also has a default value, and the jQuery API will always tell you what it is. In the case of fadeOut(), the jQuery API says:

> *Durations are given in milliseconds; higher values indicate slower animations, not faster ones. The strings 'fast' and 'slow' can be supplied to indicate durations of 200 and 600 milliseconds, respectively. If any other string is supplied, or if the duration parameter is omitted, the default duration of 400 milliseconds is used.* (http://api.jquery.com/ fadeOut/)

So if you miss out a parameter, it defaults to 400 milliseconds. Passing in "slow" was setting it to 600 milliseconds. You can also pass in a number, too. Try making it really slow. Remember, the number is milliseconds, so 3 seconds = 3000 milliseconds.

```
$(function() {
  var box = $("#box");
  box.fadeOut(3000, function() {
    alert("box finished fading out");
  });
});
```

So with fadeOut(), jQuery has the three default strings that it recognizes:

- "slow": 600 milliseconds

- "normal": 400 milliseconds (it also the default)

- "fast": 200 milliseconds

Other than that, you could pass in a value in milliseconds.

Now say you wanted to fade a box in and out continuously, maybe ten times. You'll not be surprised to learn that fadeOut() has a companion, fadeIn(), which does the exact opposite. Therefore, you can combine these two methods to get the desired effect. At least, that's what you'd do if you didn't look through the API properly.

You see, along with fadeIn() and fadeOut(), there's also fadeToggle(). This will fade in a box if it's not visible, and fade out a box if it is visible. Thus, you can use this to make things much easier. If you searched the documentation for "fade", then you have seen this method. We can't encourage you enough, especially when learning, to use the API documentation extensively.

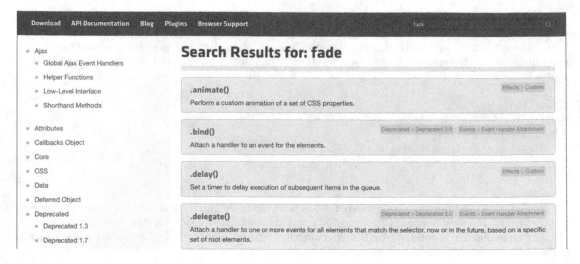

Figure 2-5. *The API documentation search results for "fade"*

So, here's what you will do:

1. Create a function that will toggle the box in and then out.

2. Store a variable that keeps count of the number of times you've done this.

3. Have a paragraph that always has its text updated to be the number of times the box has faded in and out.

The function will then call itself, making the box fade in and out once more—if the variable that keeps count is less than a certain amount.

There will be a few new things here, so be patient. By the end, you will have seen how easy jQuery makes things, which is very exciting. You are continuing from where you left off with the prior exercise, so you are not starting completely afresh.

The first thing to do is add the paragraph to your index.html page, which should look as follows:

```
<!DOCTYPE html>
<html>
  <head>
    <title>Chapter 02, Exercise 02</title>
    <script src="jquery.js"></script>
    <script src="app.js"></script>
    <link rel="stylesheet" type="text/css" href="style.css" />
  </head>
  <body>
    <div id="box">my box</div>
    <p></p>
  </body>
</html>
```

Adding an empty HTML element is not good practice, but you will learn how to learn how to avoid that problem in the near future. Edit app.js, and set up the variables you're going to use, as follows:

```
$(function() {
  var box = $("#box");
  var para = $("p");
  var i = 0;
});
```

You'll store a reference to the box, the paragraph, and the count variable i, which you set to 0. The first thing to do is make your paragraph show the value of the counter. To update the text within an element, you can use the text() method. If you call text() with no parameters, that will give you back the text. If you pass in a parameter, it will set the text to be what you pass in. Therefore, you can do para.text(i); to set the text to have the value of i.

Now you have to write the main function to perform all the toggling. Rather than do this line by line, it's easier just to look at the complete code and then walk through it. Your app.js file will look like so:

```
$(function() {
  var box = $("#box");
  var para = $("p");
  var i = 0;

  para.text(i);
  function toggleBox(i) {
    box.fadeToggle(500, function() {
      i = i + 1;
      if(i < 10) {
        para.text(i);
        toggleBox(i);
      };
    });
  };

  toggleBox(i);
});
```

Let's talk about the toggleBox() function:

```
function toggleBox(i) {
  box.fadeToggle(500, function() {
    i = i++;
    if(i < 10) {
      para.text(i);
      toggleBox(i);
    };
  });
};
```

29

The first thing you do is call `fadeToggle()`, which will fade the box in or out, depending on its current state. Just like `fadeIn()` and `fadeOut()`, give it a speed—half a second (500 in milliseconds)—and a callback function, which is executed once the box has been faded in/out. The function takes an argument, the `i` variable, which stores the number of fades that have been performed. You need this to see if you should continue fading or not.

Within the callback, do the following:

- Increment the value of `i` by 1-, the ++ operator is used, which is a shortcut for `i = i + 1`.

- If `i` < 10:

  - Set the value of the paragraph to be the current value of `i`.

  - Call `toggleBox()` again, passing in `i`.

And with that, you can refresh your page and see a box that will fade in and out five times before stopping. You'll also see the paragraph show the number of times it happened.

But hang on. Why does it show 9, and not 10? It has, in fact, faded in and out ten times. The reason is that `i` is initially set to 0, so the first time the box fades, it actually is the zero-th time it's faded. Hence, when `i` is 9, it's actually happened ten times.

It's common practice to make `count` variables start at 0, primarily due to arrays being zero-indexed, as you saw in Chapter 1. However, you might want to make the value outputted go from 1 to 10, which is easily done by changing both lines that say

```
para.text(i);
```

to

```
para.text(i+1);
```

Thus, 1–10 will display in the browser, but behind the scenes, it's using 0–9.

Summary

Wow. This has been a tough chapter, in which you've done a lot:

- Saw how to download the latest version of jQuery.

- Discovered what minified code is and why you should always use the minified jQuery version.

- Introduced some animation through `fadeIn()`, `fadeOut()`, and `fadeToggle()`.

- Used a callback function to run a piece of code once an animation has been done.

- Updated text in the DOM through the `text()` method.

- Discovered how to make code run only after the DOM is loaded by using `$(document).ready()`.

- Used the jQuery API to find the methods you want.

If you're feeling a little overawed, don't worry. This was a whistle-stop tour of some of what jQuery has to offer. The next chapter presents a more methodical look through everything jQuery has to offer by showing you how to traverse the DOM.

CHAPTER 3

Traversing the DOM

You've seen how jQuery works and how to make animated boxes fade in and out. Now it's time to take a more methodical look at the library and explore everything it can do. This chapter doesn't cover every method jQuery has to offer because a lot of methods do very similar things. There are also methods that do the exact opposite of each other. For example, in Chapter 2, after looking at how fadeOut() works, you looked only briefly at fadeIn() because it was obvious what it would do, having met fadeOut(). There is a similar situation with a lot of jQuery methods.

This chapter won't simply be a documentation of all jQuery's traversal methods, however. Efficiency is a large part of this chapter—and it will be mentioned a lot. Here's what this chapter holds:

- Selecting elements with CSS selectors and exploring which are the most efficient.

- Using jQuery pseudo-selectors.

- Exploring the variety of traversal methods that jQuery provides.

- Caching selectors and chaining methods to avoid reselecting elements.

- Avoiding more DOM work than necessary. The bottleneck of any jQuery project is always the DOM interaction. Interacting with the DOM is expensive, so the fewer times you can do it, the better.

CSS Selectors in jQuery

The beauty of jQuery, and why it became so popular, certainly involves the fact that it's so easy to use. You're probably familiar with CSS, and you know that to select an element by its ID, you use the hash symbol (#). To select an element by its class, you use a period (.), and so on. jQuery lets you use these selectors (and more) to select elements from the DOM. What's also great is that it provides backward compatibility. So even if the CSS selector you use doesn't work in IE7 and below, it will work when you use it in jQuery.

However, with great power comes great responsibility, and a lot of these selectors are highly inefficient from a computational viewpoint. The most basic way to select an element is by its ID, as follows:

```
$("#header");
$("#maincontent");
```

J. Franklin, R. Ferguson, *Beginning jQuery*, https://doi.org/10.1007/978-1-4842-3027-5_3

This way is always going to be quicker than selecting by a class or by a tag name, the other common ways; for example:

```
$(".column");
$(".header");

$("body");
$("div");
```

The reason selecting by an ID is the best way is twofold. First, JavaScript has its own mechanism for selecting by ID—document.getElementById("header")—so when jQuery detects that you've passed in an ID, it can simply call that method. Second, there should only ever be one element with any specific ID, so once it's found a result, it stops searching.

■ **Note**   It's up to you to ensure that there's only ever one instance of an ID on a page. If you do have more than one element with the same ID, JavaScript (and hence, jQuery) will only return the first one. It's invalid HTML to have an ID exist on more than one element.

If you're looking for something by a class, there could be multiple results, so JavaScript has to keep searching the entire DOM. *If you can select an element by an ID, do so.*

Another thing worth mentioning is the way jQuery deals with results of a selector. Results will return an array-like structure (it's not actually an array, but acts like one, as described in more detail shortly) regardless of whether one element is returned or fifty elements are returned. Let's say that you've got one paragraph on a page and you run $("p"). Take a look at what you get back:

```
[<p>Hey</p>]
```

If you've got a few more, you get this:

```
[<p>Hey</p>, <p>Hey</p>, <p>Hey</p>, <p>Hey</p>]
```

■ **Note**   If you're using a browser other than Google Chrome, your output may be slightly different. The preceding example shows the output from the Chrome browser developer tools. For example, in Firefox, the output is

```
[p, p, p]
```

Rest assured, the code is finding the same set of elements. It's just that the consoles output them differently.

One of the nice things about this is that you can then easily find out the number of items returned by using .length on the result, as follows, because the result acts just like a JavaScript array:

```
$("p").length; // 4
```

You can use the jQuery method $("p").size() in versions of jQuery before 1.8, but all that .size() does is return the result of using .length, so developers typically use .length.

At this stage, it might look like jQuery just returns a regular array, but it doesn't. It returns a jQuery object. This jQuery object is just like the regular objects you explored back in Chapter 1. It contains all the jQuery properties and methods alongside the elements from the selector you performed. A good way to think of it is that the jQuery object is an enhanced array. At its core, it has a list of DOM elements—but it is much more than that. Remember that when you run $("p") and get back what looks very much like an array, it's not. It's actually a jQuery object.

One of the things new users of jQuery find most confusing is the way some methods get called on every element they return, and others don't. For example, let's say you've got a list of four paragraphs and you want to give each one a class. The following will work:

```
$("p").addClass("paragraph");
```

The addClass() method is pretty self-explanatory. It simply adds a class to the elements. Notice here that this addClass() method is run on *every element in the result set*. Also notice that you do not have to loop over them. If you've got a set of elements and call a method, more often than not, jQuery will implicitly do the looping for you. This is really useful, but it can be a bit confusing, so just remember that jQuery will always loop for you if it can.

Of course, because jQuery can parse CSS selectors, you can pass it very complicated selectors, such as:

```
$("div>ul a");
$("div#main p strong");
$("div.main p>li a");
```

But the downside of those selectors is that the more complex they are, the more time they take to run, and the slower your code will execute. jQuery parses its CSS selectors from right to left, so what that last example does is

- Locates all anchor elements.

- Filters out those anchor elements not within a list item.

- Filters out all remaining elements so that the ones left are within an <li> that's an immediate child of a paragraph.

- Selects only the remaining elements that are within a class of main.

- Selects only those remaining that are within a div with that class of main.

That is a lot of work just to find some links. It's this kind of thing that you need to be wary of and keep in mind when deciding which selector to use.

Traversal Methods

Traversal methods are methods that let us "jump" around the DOM to find specific elements. A traversal method will help you get from element A to element B through a number of ways. In this section, you'll investigate what those methods are and explore how to be as efficient as possible. jQuery has a large number of traversal methods, as the documentation (http://api.jquery.com/category/traversing/) will show you.

For the rest of this chapter, we will go through the methods that we consider the most useful—and the ones you will use the most. There will be various tangents along the way to further discuss things that you need to know.

You will often have a set of elements that you want to narrow down. Perhaps you only want the first one, or the last, or perhaps you'd like a specific one from the array. You can use the eq() method to do this. Let's say that your HTML contains some paragraphs, like the following:

```
<p>Para 1</p>
<p>Para 2</p>
<p>Para 3</p>
```

Then let's say that you ran $("p"). You would get the following result:

```
[<p>Para 1</p>, <p>Para 2</p>, <p>Para 3</p>]
```

The eq() method will give back a jQuery object containing the element at a specific index. For example, $("p").eq(0) will give you the jQuery object containing your first paragraph (remember, arrays are zero-indexed). Let's say you were to run the following:

```
alert($("p").eq(0).text());
```

You'd see Para 1 because getting the first element is such a common thing to do that jQuery provides first(), which does exactly the same. It won't surprise you to learn that there's also a last() method.

Because getting the first result is so common, jQuery gives us another way of doing things. Consider the following:

```
$("p:first");
$("p:eq(0)");
```

These would both achieve the same effect. jQuery has support for a number of these pseudo-classes.

■ **Note**   jQuery supports most CSS pseudo-classes but also has a number of its own, such as :eq(0). You can find more information about pseudo-classes at: https://developer.mozilla.org/en-US/docs/Web/CSS/Pseudo-classes

---

Some pseudo-classes directly match CSS3 specification, but others (including the preceding two) do not. In the course of this chapter and this book, you will see a lot of them.

The question now becomes which one to use when jQuery offers both a pseudo-class selector and a method. We much prefer using a method to a pseudo-selector. We think they read much better and it's easier to see what's going on. This is due to the fact that when you use the method, it's not contained within the selector. This means when you're scanning through the code, the call to the method stands out more because it's not within the selector.

There's also another reason, though. Newer, more modern browsers such as Google Chrome and Mozilla Firefox support two methods that are very powerful: querySelector() and querySelectorAll(). These are powerful selection methods that can parse any CSS selector. querySelector() returns the first match for the selector, and querySelectorAll() returns all matches. jQuery will always use querySelector() and querySelectorAll() if they are available, because doing so is much quicker at getting elements with complex selectors.

If you use the $("p:first") selector, jQuery can't simply pass "p:first" to the querySelectorAll() method because ":first" is not a CSS pseudo-class. However, if you use $("p").first(), jQuery can pass the "p" selector to a native JavaScript method—getElementsByTagName() in this instance—and then call first() on the result of $("p"). *Any native method is always going to be quickest*, and so whenever you have the option to allow jQuery to use native methods, you should do so.

Further Traversal

Once you've got your initial set of elements, there's a high likelihood you're going to want to further search within them. Take the following HTML structure:

```
<div>
  <p>Paragraph <strong>one</strong></p>
  <p>Paragraph Two</p>
</div>
```

Let's say that you've first selected the <div>, and then saved that to a variable (also known as *caching*):

```
var myDiv = $("div");
```

Now let's say that you want to find all paragraphs in that <div>. jQuery offers two ways of doing this:

```
myDiv.find("p");
myDiv.children("p");
```

Or, of course, you could have originally written

```
$("div p");
```

Taking these three methods into account, which one is best? If you're going on speed alone, $("div p") will always be quickest by far in newer browsers—that is, those that support querySelector() and querySelectorAll(). If you're building a site for only these browsers, it's actually more efficient to do most of your filtering in your initial selection, so you use querySelectorAll().

If you are worrying about older and newer browsers alike, then $("div p") is often the slowest method, particularly if your selectors are more complex. That leaves two methods: find() and children(). There's an important difference between these two methods. The API describes them at http://api.jquery.com/ category/traversing/ children() is described as "Get the children of each element in the set of matched elements, optionally filtered by a selector." find() is described as "Get the descendants of each element in the current set of matched elements, filtered by a selector, jQuery object, or element."

The key difference is in the third word of each description. The first method will get the *children* of each element, and the second method gets the *descendants*. Take this diagram:

```
div
- p
- p
- - strong
- - - a
```

Here, the paragraphs are *children* of the div. However the paragraphs, the <strong>, and the anchor are all *descendants* of the div. Children are *direct descendants* only, whereas *descendants* means everything within that element, regardless of what level it's on.

In this situation, examine the following structure:

```
<div>
  <p>Paragraph <strong>one</strong></p>
  <p>Paragraph Two</p>
</div>
```

You should use `children()`, not `find`. The reason is that `find()` will search *every level of the DOM* to try and find a match, whereas `children()` will *only search the immediate level of the element* to find a match. So, when you only want immediate descendants, as in the example, `children()` is going to be quicker. Admittedly, it's a marginal speed difference, but it's only going to do what you need it to do—whereas `find` would do much more—so it makes sense to stick to `children()`. It also shows that you're only selecting immediate descendants, making your code read better.

With the two methods, `children()` and `find()`, you're not limited to passing in a tag. They, along with all traversal methods akin to them, take any CSS selector, just like the ones you might pass in to the initial jQuery object through `$()`, such as:

```
$("div").find("p>strong");
```

This will return all `strong` elements that are direct children of paragraphs, where those paragraphs exist within a `div`.

Another very useful method is `siblings()`, which gets all the siblings of the current element, as you might expect. Take this structure:

```
<div>
  <p class="first-paragraph">Paragraph 1</p>
  <p>Paragraph 2</p>
  <p>Paragraph <strong>3</strong></p>
</div>
```

Running `$("div").siblings()` will give you no results. This is because the `<div>` is the only element at that level. To get all the siblings of the first paragraph, you could do the following:

```
$(".first-paragraph").siblings();
```

This would give a result set containing the other two paragraphs, but *not* the initial paragraph. If you wanted to add the initial paragraph to the set of elements so that you have both the element's siblings and the original element, you could use `.add()`, which can be used to add other elements to an existing set. For example, consider using the following:

```
$(".main").add(".paragraphs");
```

It would leave you with a result set of elements with a class of `"main"` and also those with a class of `"paragraphs"`. So in the example, you could do the following:

```
$(".first-paragraph").siblings().add(".first-paragraph");
```

But this isn't very efficient. Notice that you're running the selector twice. This means that you're searching the DOM twice, which is not good at all. Thankfully, jQuery provides `andSelf()`, which is an easier way to do this. It takes the set of elements from the previous selection and adds it to the current selection:

```
$(".first-paragraph").siblings().andSelf();
```

This gives a set that includes the `siblings()` and the initial paragraph. `andSelf()` is not a method you will find yourself using that frequently, but it's a very useful one to know. With your DOM structure, there's actually another way you can get the siblings of the first paragraph:

```
$(".first-paragraph").nextAll();
```

nextAll() gets all the siblings that are *after* the current element. So, with this HTML, it is as follows:

```
<div>
  <p>Paragraph 1</p>
  <p class="second">Paragraph 2</p>
  <p>Paragraph 3</p>
</div>
```

Running $(".second").nextAll(); gives just one element back—the third paragraph. Running $(".second").siblings() gives two elements—the first paragraph and the last. So nextAll() gets all siblings that are after the current element in the DOM structure. There's also the opposite method, prevAll(), which gets all siblings before the current element. You've also got prev() and next(), which get the sibling next to the current element—either the one before the current element in the case of prev(), or the one after the current element in the case of next().

Chaining Methods

You may have noticed that the preceding example *chained* two methods together, like so

```
$(".first-paragraph").siblings().andSelf();
```

This is one of jQuery's key features. Methods can be called one after another and be chained together. Any methods that return a jQuery object can be chained. To tell if a method returns the jQuery object, check the top-right corner of its jQuery API documentation (see Figure 3-1).

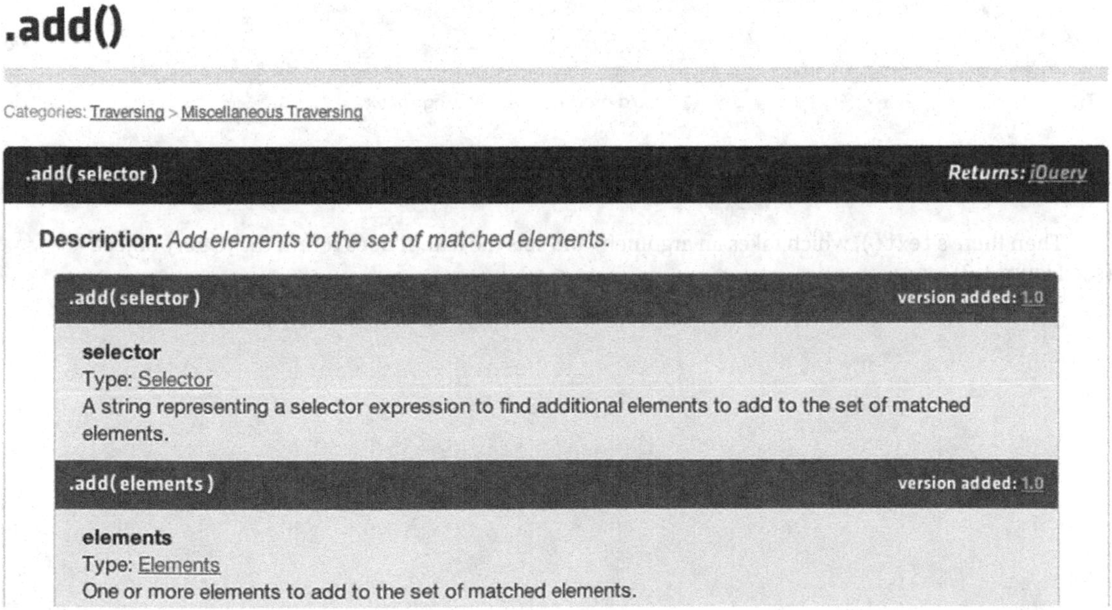

.add()

Categories: Traversing > Miscellaneous Traversing

.add(selector)	Returns: *jQuery*

Description: *Add elements to the set of matched elements.*

.add(selector)	version added: 1.0

selector
Type: Selector
A string representing a selector expression to find additional elements to add to the set of matched elements.

.add(elements)	version added: 1.0

elements
Type: Elements
One or more elements to add to the set of matched elements.

Figure 3-1. The top-right corner of the documentation shows that this method returns "jQuery", meaning it can be chained

The top-right corner of the screenshot shows that this method returns jQuery. This means that the method can be chained.

There are methods that either can be chained or cannot be chained, depending on how they are used. One such method is one you saw back in Chapter 2, text(). If you call text() with no arguments, it will return the text of the element. However, if you pass it some text, it will set the text of that element, and will then return a jQuery object. The documentation for text() shows this. There are two different entries.

The first is for text() on its own, which returns the text. You can see that the documentation denotes that it returns a string (see Figure 3-2).

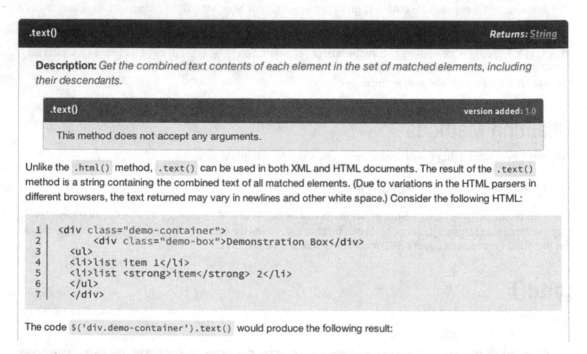

Figure 3-2. *This method cannot be chained because it returns a string*

Then there's text(), which takes an argument and sets the text. It does return the jQuery object (see Figure 3-3).

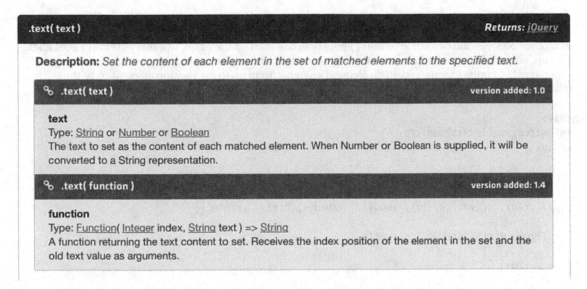

.text(text)   Returns: jQuery

Description: *Set the content of each element in the set of matched elements to the specified text.*

∞ .text(text)   version added: 1.0

text
Type: String or Number or Boolean
The text to set as the content of each matched element. When Number or Boolean is supplied, it will be
converted to a String representation.

∞ .text(function)   version added: 1.4

function
Type: Function(Integer index, String text) => String
A function returning the text content to set. Receives the index position of the element in the set and the
old text value as arguments.

Figure 3-3. When you use .text() to set the text, it returns jQuery, so it can be chained

The general rule of thumb is that any method that doesn't explicitly return something other than a set of elements can be chained.

Chaining is a good way to avoid selecting elements more than once, as follows:

```
$("div").fadeOut();
$("div").css("color", "red");
$("div").text("hello world");
```

Instead of doing that and running $("div") three times, you could do this:

```
$("div").fadeOut().css("color", "red").text("hello world");
```

White space isn't important here, so if you want to split these onto multiple lines, feel free. We often do it like so:

```
$("div")
  .fadeOut()
  .css("color", "red")
  .text("hello world");
```

Just be careful that you don't miss any dots between methods, and remember that the semicolon only goes at the end. If you're not into chaining, you might prefer to cache the selection, as you've already seen:

```
var div = $("div");
div.fadeOut();
div.css("color", "red");
div.text("hello world");
```

So far, you've used `children()` and `find()` to traverse further down the DOM structure, but of course there are also functions for doing the exact opposite. These are called `parent()` and `parents()`. The key difference between the two is that `parent()` goes only one level up the DOM, whereas `parents()` goes all the way up. You can find the definitions for these functions (as with all) on the jQuery site.

`parents()` quite literally gets all an element's parents, right up to the very top element. Take the following HTML structure:

```
<div>
<p><strong>Hello</strong></p>
</div>
```

The result of `$("strong").parents()` is

```
[<p>...</p>, <div>...</div>, <body>...</body>,<html>...</html>]
```

The result of `$("strong").parent()` is

```
[<p>...</p>]
```

Because `parents()` traverses the entire DOM, you'll nearly always want to pass it some selector, simply because it's rarely ever useful for `.parents()` to give back the body and html elements. However, sometimes you may want all the parents up to the body element, so something you often need to do is filter out the set of elements that `parents()` returns. There are two ways of doing this. The first is to use jQuery filters. Earlier you used the `:eq` selector and the `.eq()` method to filter your results down to one result. That is one of jQuery's filtering methods, which are all documented in the API (`http://api.jquery.com/category/traversing/filtering/`).

The method that interests us right now is `not()`. We will also cover the rest—some in this chapter and some elsewhere in the book. `not()` does exactly what you'd expect—it filters results. If you want to remove the body and html elements from your `parents()` call, it's as easy as this:

```
$("strong").parents().not("html, body");
```

This takes all the parents and filters out the html and body tags. This works because `not()` takes a CSS selector. You are effectively telling jQuery to filter out elements that match the CSS selector `"html, body"`. And of course, this selector matches the html and body elements. You can also use the pseudo-class `:not`, much like you could use `:eq`, but as explained earlier, using the method is preferable to the pseudo-class (and it's easier to read), so that's while you'll see for the rest of this book.

There is, however, a much better way to do what you want, and that's to use `parentsUntil()`. With `parentsUntil()`, your code is much simpler. Remember, `parentsUntil()` gets all elements up to but *not including* the one your selector matches. Now that you know of this method, all you have to do is the following:

```
$("strong").parentsUntil("body");
```

This gives the desired result. It is a strong trend with jQuery. If something seems a bit long-winded, there's a high chance that there's an easier way to do it.

Two filters that are very useful are the `:even` and `:odd` filters. Combining them with the `filter()` method, which takes a filter and returns the ones that pass, you can easily apply background colors to rows to make the table appear striped. Here's a simple table to use:

```
<!DOCTYPE html>
<html>
  <head>
    <title>Chapter 03, Exercise 01</title>
```

```
     <script src="jquery.js"></script>
     <script src="app.js"></script>
     <link rel="stylesheet" type="text/css" href="style.css" />
   </head>
   <body>
     <table>
       <tr><td>Jack</td><td>Franklin</td></tr>
       <tr><td>Stuart</td><td>Robson</td></tr>
       <tr><td>Rob</td><td>Hawkes</td></tr>
       <tr><td>Alex</td><td>Older</td></tr>
     </table>
   </body>
</html>
```

The following just gives the tables some borders to clearly define the rows:

```
table {
  border-collapse: collapse;
}
tr {
  border-left: 1px solid grey;
  border-right: 1px solid grey;
  border-bottom: 1px solid grey;
}

td {
  padding: 10px;
}
```

You can see the results in Figure 3-4.

Jack	Franklin
Stuart	Robson
Rob	Hawkes
Alex	Older

Figure 3-4. *The plain table ready to apply the striped effect*

Here's the app.js file:

```
$(function() {
  var rows = $("tr");
  rows.filter(":even").css("background", "red");
  rows.filter(":odd").css("background", "blue");
});
```

This gives the result shown in Figure 3-5 (which certainly won't be winning any design awards).

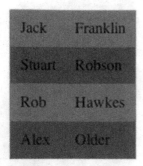

Figure 3-5. *The table once the code has run*

The `app.js` file does three very simple things:

- Stores the result of `$("tr")` to a variable, `rows`.

- Filters the even rows and colors them red.

- Filters the odd rows and colors them blue.

This is the `css()` method, but it's pretty simple. When passed two arguments—a property and a value—it will set the CSS value of the elements in the set. This very simple example shows you the power of jQuery filters.

Further Filtering

If jQuery's built-in filters are not enough, it also provides a mechanism that allows you to filter by anything you want. You briefly saw the `filter()` method in action when you filtered for even rows with `filter("even")`. You can also pass `filter()` a function that will evaluate each element in a set and return only those that match a certain condition.

In your `index.html` page, add four paragraphs so that it looks like so:

```
<!DOCTYPE html>
<html>
  <head>
    <title>Chapter 03, Exercise 02</title>
    <script src="jquery.js"></script>
    <script src="app.js"></script>
    <link rel="stylesheet" type="text/css" href="style.css" />
  </head>
  <body>
    <p><strong>Jack</strong> Franklin</p>
    <p><strong>John</strong> Hammelink</p>
    <p><strong>Richard</strong> Quick</p>
    <p>Will Hammil</p>
  </body>
</html>
```

Get rid of everything previously in your style.css; you won't need any styling.

Now, let's say that you want to filter for only the paragraphs that have a <strong> tag and give them a red background. The first thing you want to do is get all the paragraphs and store them in a variable, like so:

```
$(function() {
  var ps = $("p");
});
```

When you pass filter() a function, it expects this function to return true or false. filter() runs once for each element, and will *keep elements when the function you pass in evaluates to* true. It will get rid of elements that make the function evaluate to false.

Within this function, you have access to the current element through the this keyword, mentioned in Chapter 1. The this keyword is a special variable in JavaScript that you can use often to reference the current item you're working with. To gain access to the current element you're working with but wrapped in a jQuery object, you can simply run $(this).

To filter out all elements without a strong element within, you need to check if the paragraph contains any. There are two bits of information that will get that result:

- You can get all strong elements within an element through $("p").children("strong");

- You can see how many elements are in the result set by adding .length, like so: $("p").children("strong").length;

So, for a paragraph to contain strong elements, the following must be true:

```
$("p").children("strong").length > 0;
```

This expression, which can return true or false, is what you'll pass into your filter function, like so:

```
$(function() {
  var ps = $("p");

  var strongPs = ps.filter(function() {
    return $(this).children("strong").length > 0;
  });

  strongPs.css("background", "red");
});
```

You get the desired outcome, shown in Figure 3-6.

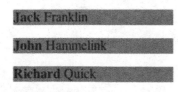

Jack Franklin

John Hammelink

Richard Quick

Will Hammil

Figure 3-6. Three of the four paragraphs, the ones with a <strong> inside, are given a red background

I'm sure you can imagine that the filter() method, when passed a function, is incredibly powerful. You could filter for absolutely anything that you want, as long as you can evaluate it to true.

There's one way you could simplify the code. The filter() method still returns the jQuery object, which means *it can be chained.* This means that you can shorten the code a little, as follows:

```
$(function() {
  var ps = $("p");

  ps.filter(function() {
    return $(this).children("strong").length > 0;
  }).css("background", "red");
});
```

Here you are using a ps variable, but only referring to it once; get rid of it so that you're left with the following:

```
$(function() {
  $("p").filter(function() {
    return $(this).children("strong").length > 0;
  }).css("background", "red");
});
```

Much better!

Summary

This has been the most intense chapter yet and you covered a lot of new ground. All the methods covered will be used throughout the book, so if there's something you're not too sure about, don't worry—there are going to be a lot more opportunities to use these methods. With jQuery, a lot is practice, so we suggest you go through and write some code yourself. Try it out. Remember to use the API documentation—it really is fantastic. In the next chapter you'll start to manipulate the DOM with jQuery.

■ ■ ■

CHAPTER 4

DOM Manipulation with jQuery

So now you know a fair amount about jQuery and what it can do. You know how to select elements, how to make sure your code only runs after the DOM is loaded, and plenty more. You've also taken a look at animations and done some basic manipulation by changing colors of elements using the `css()` method. What you might not have realized is that animations are manipulation. Previously, you used `fadeIn()`/`fadeOut()` to manipulate the opacity of an element over a period of time. This chapter will focus entirely on manipulation of elements, including:

- Changing CSS styles with the `css()` method
- More animation as you meet jQuery's `animate()` method
- Inserting, removing, and moving elements around the DOM
- Editing element attributes with `attr()`
- A myriad of manipulation methods that jQuery provides

On your way through, you'll take regular pauses and small tangents to examine best practices. As mentioned in Chapter 3, DOM manipulation is often a huge bottleneck in web sites, so you should try to do it as little as possible. There are many tricks and ways to limit the time spent on the DOM, and we'll mention these as you go through the chapter.

Chapter 3 also pointed out that the jQuery API leaves you well covered when it comes to learning the API methods for manipulation (`http://api.jquery.com/category/manipulation/`), so feel free to refer to that at any time.

CSS

jQuery's `css()` method is very powerful. There are actually three primary ways that you'll work with it. The first is when determining the value of an element's property. Simply pass it one parameter—the property whose value you want to know:

```
$("div").css("width");
```

```
$("div").css("margin-right");
```

```
$("div").css("color");
```

It's important to note that if you have a set of more than one element and you call `css()`, you'll get the result as if `css()` was called on just the first element. Another important note is that you can't use shorthand. For example, this won't work:

```
$("div").css("margin");
```

© Jack Franklin, Russ Ferguson 2017
J. Franklin, R. Ferguson, *Beginning jQuery*, https://doi.org/10.1007/978-1-4842-3027-5_4

■ **Note** If you're using css() to get the width, you might want to look at jQuery's width(), innerWidth(), and outerWidth() methods. While css("width") will return a string like "200px", the width methods always return an integer value. If you're performing any calculations based on width, it's much easier to get it as an integer from the start rather than having to get a string and convert it.

You can also use CSS to set values. To set just one value, pass in a property and a value as separate parameters. You used this in Chapter 3.

```
$("div").css("color", "red");
```

```
$("div").css("border", "1px solid red");
```

What's more useful is that the css() method also accepts an object of key-value pairs that map CSS properties to the values you want to set. For example:

```
$("div").css({
  "background" : "red",
  "margin-left": "200px",
  "color": "black"
});
```

That is a much quicker way to set CSS properties. However, if you find yourself doing this often, it's quite possible that you should actually create a new CSS class to have those properties, and then simply add that class to the element with jQuery. This means jQuery does less manipulation, as it only has to add a class. To add a class, simply use the addClass() method:

```
$("div").addClass("column");
```

There's also removeClass():

```
$("div").removeClass("column");
```

If you want to check if an element has a particular class, there's hasClass():

```
$("div").hasClass("column");
```

That will return true or false. If you want to add a class to something, you can do it regardless of whether the element already has that class or not. jQuery is smart enough to sort all that out for you. There's no need to do this:

```
if( !$("div").hasClass("main") ) {
  $("div").addClass("main");
};
```

Simply call addClass(). Similarly, there's no need to check whether an element has a class before you remove that class. Both these methods can take multiple arguments:

```
$("div").addClass("one two three");
$("div").removeClass("four five six");
```

48

And in a situation where you'd like to add a class if the element doesn't have it—but remove that same class if the element does have it—jQuery also has you covered:

```
$("div").toggleClass("main");
```

If the elements in that set have the class, they will have it removed; but if they do not have it, it will be added.

There are also some things you could use the css() method for that jQuery provides better alternatives to. For example, to hide an element, you might change its CSS "display" property to "none":

```
$("div").css("display", "none");
```

And then you could show it again:

```
$("div").css("display", "block");
```

But what if before you hid it, its "display" property was set to "inline" or "inline-block"? jQuery solves this by providing two methods: hide() and show(). What's great about them is that when you use hide() to hide an element, jQuery not only hides it but also remembers its "display" property. Then, when you call show() on that element, it sets the display property back to what it was previously. So, for showing and hiding elements, do as follows, rather than using the css() method:

```
$("div").hide();
```

```
$("div").show();
```

animate() and Animation Convenience Methods

You've already discovered animations, but until now, you haven't met the main animation function jQuery uses: animate(). From looking at its documentation (http://api.jquery.com/animate/), you'd think it's very complex and difficult to use, but in reality, it's fantastic. Even though you haven't met this method yet, all the animation methods you've used so far, including fadeIn() and fadeOut(), use animate(). jQuery provides these methods, known as *convenience methods*, to save you some typing. Here's the code that implements fadeIn() from the jQuery source:

```
function (speed, easing, callback) {
    return this.animate(props, speed, easing, callback);
}
```

All it does is pass on the parameters you pass in to the animate() method. If you didn't have the fade methods, here's how you'd fade an element out:

```
$("div").animate({
  "opacity": 0
}, 1000);
```

That would animate the div's opacity down to 0 over 1000 milliseconds, or 1 second. Typing that every time would get frustrating, so the convenience methods like fadeIn() are implemented to save you some typing. There are many more convenience methods, not just for animation, but also general ones. You'll meet a lot throughout the book.

The general usage of animate() works very similarly to the css() method: it takes an object of properties and values to set. The second parameter is the time it takes to animate the properties. The third is a callback function that works exactly like the ones you passed into the fade methods earlier in the book. The following snippet passes in three arguments to animate(). The first is an object of key-value pairs containing properties and the values you wish them to end up as; the second is the time in milliseconds (again, 1 second = 1000 milliseconds); and the third is the callback function. This function will be executed as soon as the animation is complete.

```
$("div").animate({
  'width' : 200
}, 2000, function() {
  alert("Div is now 200px wide!");
});
```

Another common animation is animating the height of elements, typically to hide them by sliding them "up" so they have a height of 0—and are effectively hidden—or sliding them "down" to give height, thus revealing the elements to the user. By animating the height to 0, you are effectively hiding the div:

```
$("div").animate({
  'height' : 0
}, 2000);
```

But as this is so common, jQuery provides three methods to make things easier:

- slideUp()

- slideDown()

- slideToggle()

These methods animate elements by height. slideUp() animates an element to a height of 0, creating the effect that the element slides up the page, with its height getting smaller and smaller until it disappears. slideDown() does the reverse, animating an element's height to a specific value. Finally, slideToggle() slides an element either up or down, based on the state it's in when you call it. If you call slideToggle() on an element that has height 0, it slides it down and reveals it. If you call slideToggle() on an element that is visible, it slides it up.

Now take a look at an example to see how you might use these methods. You will create a "box" on your page with a quick bit of CSS, and then see how the slide methods affect this element.

Create a new folder to house these files, and create index.html, app.js, and style.css. Add the basic HTML you've used for all the previous exercises (we suggest you simply copy and paste an old exercise and rename it). Your index.html should look like this:

```
<!DOCTYPE html>
<html>
  <head>
    <title>Chapter 04, Exercise 01</title>
    <script src="jquery.js"></script>
    <script src="app.js"></script>
    <link rel="stylesheet" type="text/css" href="style.css" />
  </head>
  <body>
    <div id="box">
      <p>A box</p>
    </div>
  </body>
</html>
```

Quickly whip up some styling:

```css
#box {
  width: 200px;
  height: 200px;
  background: red;
}
```

and have your app.js blank, ready to be filled with some animation awesomeness:

```js
$(function() {
});
```

Now add a call to slideUp() after selecting the div:

```js
$(function() {
  $("#box").slideUp(2000);
});
```

Refresh the page, and you'll see the box slide out of view over a period of 2 seconds. Remember, all that slideUp() does is call the animate() method; it's just a nice shortcut.

Now change your app.js file so it looks like this:

```js
$(function() {
  var i = 0;
  while( i < 10 ) {
    $("#box").slideToggle(2000);
    i++;
  };
});
```

When you refresh the page, you'll see the box slide up, and down, and up, and so on. It will slide ten times. The preceding code contains a loop that runs when the variable i is less than 10. With i initially set to 0, this makes sure the loop will run ten times. Within this loop, you call slideToggle(), which slides a box up if it's visible and slides a box down if it's not. The line below that, i++, increments the value of i by one.

Attributes and Properties

To get and set attributes of DOM elements, jQuery provides the attr() method. This works just like the css() method. There are three ways to do things:

- $("div").attr("id") to get the value of the ID attribute

- $("div").attr("id", "main") to set the value of the ID attribute to "main"

- $("div").attr({
    "id" : "main",
    "rel" : "one"

  }); to set multiple attributes at once

But there's also prop(), which deals with *properties*. attr() deals with *attributes*. For example, given a piece of HTML like so:

```
<input type="checkbox" checked="checked" />
```

That checked attribute indicates whether the check box should be checked or not *when the page loads*. It does not update itself when the user interacts with it. That is managed through the checked *property*, which updates when the user ticks or unticks the check box. This is an example of when you should use prop() over attr(). Attributes are what you can *see in the HTML*, whereas properties are used "behind the scenes." If you'd like to read more on this, a jQuery blog post at http://blog.jquery.com/2011/05/12/jquery-1-6-1-released/ is a good place to start. It has a thorough explanation of the differences and when you should use one or the other.

In our experience, *the vast majority of the time, you can (and should) use* attr(). Even when you use attr() in a place where prop() would have been preferred, attr() will simply call prop() for you. This doesn't mean that you should simply always use attr()—there are speed gains to be had from using prop(). Throughout this book, you'll see times where prop() should be used, particularly later in the book when you look at working with HTML forms.

When setting properties on the window or document objects, you should *always* use prop(), simply because the window and document objects are not HTML elements—because there are no attributes on them.

Here prop() is used exactly the same as attr(), so there's no need to demonstrate how it's used. The key takeaway from this section is the difference between them. It can be a confusing difference that takes a while to pick up. Don't worry if you need to reread this section.

text() and html()

If you want to update some text within an element, the best way to do it is by using the text() method. Like many other jQuery methods, it will return the value of the text when called without arguments; but when called with an argument, it will set the text of an element. For example:

```
<p>Hello</p>
$("p").text(); //Hello
$("p").text("Hey");
$("p").text(); //Hey
$("p").text("<strong>Hey</strong");
$("p").text(); //<strong>Hey</strong>
```

When you pass in HTML to the text() method, it is automatically escaped for you. This means that jQuery replaces the symbol "<" with its HTML entity, which is "<". The browser then displays this as the "<" symbol, but it's not HTML, just plain text. The browser also escapes ">" to ">". This means you'll see the text "Hey", and not the word "Hey" wrapped in strong tags.

The strong tag is escaped, so it's not applied. This is where html() comes in. html() works exactly the same as text() but will not escape any HTML within it. This means that in the preceding example, if you use html() instead of text(), you'll see that it's interpreted as HTML, which means the strong tag is not escaped, and hence you'll see the word "Hey", which should now be bold.

You shouldn't get into the practice of inserting complex HTML via these methods, though. jQuery provides a myriad of options for inserting into the DOM, which you will see shortly.

Removing Elements from the DOM

jQuery has a number of ways to remove elements from the DOM, which you can find at http://api.jquery.com/category/manipulation/dom-removal/.

Let's start with the one that seems the most obvious: remove(). It removes the set of elements from the DOM but also removes anything else associated with it—such as events. So say you've got some code that runs when an element is clicked, but you then remove that element and insert it back into the DOM somewhere else. In this instance, you'll have to reassign that code to run when that element is clicked. Running remove() completely gets rid of anything associated with it.

Using remove() returns the entire set of elements that match the selector, *not* just the set of elements it just removed. This is an easy mistake to make. Given this HTML structure:

```
<div>
  <p>hey</p>
</div>
```

and this JavaScript:

```
$(function() {
  var p = $("p").remove();
  console.log(p);
});
```

the following is logged. Please note that these examples are generated from the Google Chrome developer console. If you use a different one, you may get different outputs. For example, the Firefox console will simply show [p] for the next example. Don't worry about this—it's just how each browser outputs results to its console.

```
[<p>Hey</p>]
```

This would make you presume that it gives back what it removed. However, if you have this HTML:

```
<div>
  <p>hey</p>

  <p class="remove">hello</p>
</div>
```

and this JavaScript:

```
$(function() {
  var p = $("p").remove(".remove");
  console.log(p);
});
```

you get both the paragraphs logged:

```
[<p>hey</p>, <p class="remove">hello</p>]
```

Notice how you are able to pass a selector to the remove() method to filter the results. Here we have selected only elements with a class of "remove" from the selection, $("p"). We could have used $(".remove").remove() and achieved the same thing in this situation.

You might be asking how would you insert that element back into the DOM to move it from one place in the DOM to another, if you can't get what you just removed. We will discuss how to add that element back into the DOM shortly.

If you want to remove an element from the DOM but not its associations, there's detach(),which works exactly the same as remove(), except it won't remove things like code that runs when the element is clicked, despite the fact that you've taken the element out of the DOM. So if you were to reinsert an element you'd removed with detach(), any event handlers would still fire. remove(), on the other hand, completely removes the element and all event handlers.

At times, you might want to remove everything within an element but not the element itself. This is where empty() comes in. Taking the HTML structure used previously:

```
<div>
  <p>hey</p>
  <p class="remove">hello</p>
</div>
```

running this piece of JavaScript:

```
$(function() {
  var d = $("div").empty();
  console.log(d);
});
```

logs the following (once again, if you're in a different browser, you might get slightly different output):

```
[<div></div>]
```

The div is completely emptied. A very important note on empty() is that it will also *remove text within the element*. This is because, technically, text is a DOM node and empty() removes all nodes from the element.

The final method for removing an element is unwrap(), which does roughly the opposite of empty(). empty() takes an element and removes its children, whereas unwrap() takes an element and removes its parent element. Given the following:

```
<div>
  <p>hey</p>
</div>
```

and the following JavaScript:

```
$(function() {
  $("p").unwrap();
  console.log($("body").html());
});
```

once you've called unwrap(), you then use the html() method, which when called without any arguments returns a string that is the HTML within that element. The result, predictably, is

```
[<p>Hey</p>]
```

54

unwrap() simply removes the parent of the element it's called on.

Creating New Elements

Before getting to inserting new content into the DOM, you first need to look at how to create a new object. The easiest way is to create a string of HTML. Most of the insertion methods you're about to see will happily accept this:

```
var newParagraph = "<p>Hello</p>";
```

However, this can get complicated very quickly if you're inserting structures that are more complex. There's nothing wrong with using a string for a quick addition like the preceding one; but for anything more complex, you should create it like so:

```
var newDiv = $("<div></div>", {
  "text": "Hello",
  "class": "newDiv",
  "title": "Hello"
});
```

That's the best way to create complicated elements, which have a lot of attributes to set. You call jQuery on an empty element, and then pass in an object that maps properties to values. Notice that you can also use jQuery methods. The preceding example denotes a property "text" and gives it a value of "Hello", which jQuery then converts and uses its text() method to set the text to "Hello". You can then save this new element to a variable so that you can insert it into the DOM. Let's do that now!

Inserting into the DOM

At last, you're here! It's taken a while, but you can finally look at how to put things into the DOM. So far, you've manipulated existing elements and removed them, but without adding things back in. jQuery offers a huge range of ways to insert things into the DOM, so you'll take a look at a few of the most popular ones. We will also discuss efficiency, because doing things inefficiently when the DOM is involved is computationally very expensive. If you take a look at the jQuery docs, there are three categories of DOM insertion methods:

- **DOM Insertion, Around**: These methods let you insert elements around existing ones.

- **DOM Insertion, Inside**: These methods let you insert elements within existing ones.

- **DOM Insertion, Outside**: These methods let you insert elements outside existing ones that are completely separate.

We'll discuss each of these categories. There are too many methods to discuss them all, but as always, we'll pick the ones that we tend to use the most often and the ones we see others frequently using.

DOM Insertion, Around

There are just three methods within this section. You'll remember that you looked at `unwrap()` and how it was used to remove the parent of an element. The "around" methods all do the opposite of this: they wrap new elements around existing ones. There are three methods:

- `wrap()`
- `wrapAll()`
- `wrapInner()`

You'll most often use `wrap()`, but the other methods are also useful, so you'll take a look at them, starting with `wrap()`. For all examples using `wrap()`, you will use this HTML structure:

```
<div>
  <p>hey</p>
</div>
```

The simplest use is to pass `wrap()` a string:

```
$("p").wrap("<div></div>");
```

which gives you:

```
<div>
  <div>
    <p>Hey</p>
  </div>
</div>
```

This has wrapped a new `div` element around the paragraph element.

You can actually shorten that a little. When passing in an HTML string that is a new empty element, you can do the following simply to save a few characters:

```
$("p").wrap("<div />");
```

Of course, you can also wrap elements by creating new ones via the method you saw in the previous section when you created a new element by passing in the HTML string and then an object of properties. You can then call `wrap()`, passing in the new object that you just created. For example:

```
var newDiv = $("<div />", {
  "class" : "Hello",
  "text": "Hey"
});
$("p").wrap(newDiv);
```

gives you:

```
<div> <div class="Hello">Hey<p>hey</p></div> </div>
```

You can see your paragraph has been wrapped with the new `div`.

`wrapAll()` does something similar: it takes every element in the set and wraps them all in the new element. So, with the preceding example, you could have used `wrapAll()` to gain the same effect. If you have two paragraphs and call `wrapAll()`, they both become wrapped within a `div`. For example:

```
<div>
  <p>Hey</p>
  <p>Hello</p>
</div>
```

```
$("p").wrapAll("<div />");
```

gives you:

```
<div>
  <div><p>Hey</p><p>Hello</p></div>
</div>
```

This is useful if you need to add a new containing element around a whole group of elements.

The final wrap function is `wrapInner()`, which wraps the contents of each element in the new element. For example, the preceding HTML structure running

```
$("p").wrapInner("<strong />");
```

gives you:

```
<div> <p><strong>Hey</strong></p> <p><strong>Hello</strong></p> </div>
```

DOM Insertion, Inside

DOM Insertion, Inside methods let you take an existing element in the DOM and add elements within it. The jQuery documentation (`http://api.jquery.com/category/manipulation/dom-insertion-inside/`) sums this up best: "These methods allow us to insert new content inside an existing element."

There are six methods here (you've already met two of them):

- `append()`
- `appendTo()`
- `html()`
- `prepend()`
- `prependTo()`
- `text()`

You've already seen and used `html()` and `text()`, so we'll skip over those in this section. You can probably guess that `prepend()` and `append()` (as well as the "To" versions) do very similar things; there's not too much to go over here. You may find yourself using `append()` and `prepend()` on a regular basis, so it's important that you understand these examples.

append() is pretty simple. You pass it a new element, or some HTML, and it adds that onto the end of *each* element in the set. This is best explained with an example, so imagine that you have three empty div elements:

```
<div></div>
<div></div>
<div></div>
```

and run:

```
var p = $("<p />", {
  "text" : "Hello"
});
$("div").append(p)
```

Consequently, the DOM will now look like so, with each div containing a new paragraph:

```
<div><p>Hello</p></div>
<div><p>Hello</p></div>
<div><p>Hello</p></div>
```

It's important to note that append() adds content at the *end*, after all the other elements in that element. From here, you can probably guess that prepend() will insert elements at the *beginning*, before all other elements. Taking a div with some content already in it, running prepend() would insert the new element *before* that content, whereas append() would put it *after* the content. Take this div from the preceding HTML, for example:

```
<div><p>Hello</p></div>
```

If you then run the same jQuery snippet, but change the text in the paragraph:

```
var p = $("<p />", {
  "text" : "Howdy"
});
$("div").append(p)
```

you will see:

```
<div><p>Hello</p><p>Howdy</p></div>
```

But if you instead run:

```
var p = $("<p />", {
  "text" : "Howdy"
});
$("div").prepend(p)
```

you will see:

```
<div><p>Howdy</p><p>Hello</p></div>
```

prependTo() and appendTo() are simply a way of writing the code differently. With append(), you select the element and then add content to it, whereas appendTo() performs in the reverse. For example:

```
<p>Howdy</p>
```

```
$("<strong>hello</strong>").appendTo("p")
```

gives you:

```
<p>Howdy<strong>hello</strong></p>
```

appendTo() takes one argument, which can be any CSS selector or a jQuery object already. So you could use the following to get the same result:

```
var p = $("p");
$("<strong>Hello</strong>").appendTo(p);
```

These also work just fine with prependTo (the two methods work exactly the same in this respect). For example:

```
var p = $("p");
$("<strong>Hello</strong>").prependTo(p);
```

results in the following:

```
<p><strong>Hello</strong>Howdy</p>
```

DOM Insertion, Outside

These methods let you insert content outside other elements. There are four methods here, but really, there are only two because they are exact opposites, just like prepend() and append():

- after()
- before()
- insertAfter()
- insertBefore()

after() is used to insert content after the elements in your set. For example:

```
<div><p>Hello</p></div>
```

```
$("p").after("<span>Hey</span>");
```

would give you:

```
<div><p>Hello</p><span>Hey</span></div>
```

And if you were to do:

```
$("p").before("<span>Hey</span>");
```

you'd get:

```
<div><span>Hey</span><p>Hello</p></div>
```

From here, based on what you just did in the last section, you can probably guess what `insertAfter()` does. It is simply a different syntax:

```
$("<span>Hey</span>").insertAfter("p");
$("<span>Hey</span>").insertBefore("p");
```

We tend to use this syntax—`prependTo()`, `insertAfter()`, and so forth—much more than the other syntax. This is mainly because using a method where the thing you want to insert is "first" in the code, you can create new elements and insert them much easier. For example, this:

```
$("<p />", {
  "text": "Hello"
}).insertAfter("p");
```

is much nicer than this:

```
var p = $("<p />", {
  "text": "Hello"
})
$("p").after(p);
```

We will tend to use `insertAfter()`, `appendTo()`, and so on in further exercises in this book, but feel free to swap them around if you prefer to do things that way.

Efficient DOM Insertion

Before moving on to events in Chapter 5, we'd like to take a moment to discuss efficiency. As we have mentioned, *DOM manipulation is expensive.* Relative to most of the JavaScript you'll write, removing, manipulating, or inserting DOM elements is going to be the slowest part. The most common example in which we see people using it inefficiently is when they are inserting lots of content in a loop. Suppose that you want to generate an unordered list of the numbers 1 to 10, and you decide performing this in a loop is a good way to do it. Here's how you might do it. Create a new folder for this exercise and set up the usual structure, an `index.html` file and an `app.js` file that just contains

```
$(function() {
});
```

You can add a `style.css` for styling if you like. Here's an initial attempt at making a list:

```
$(function() {
  var i = 0;
  var newUl = $("<ul />").appendTo("body");
  while( i < 10 ) {
```

```
$("<li />", {
    "text" : i+1
}).appendTo(newUl);
i++;
    }
});
```

Here are the steps:

1. Create a new unordered list and add it to the <body> element.

2. Then loop ten times. Within the loop, create a new list item and add it to the unordered list.

3. Set the text value to i+1, so the list items read 1–10 and not 0–9.

You might think that this is fine, but in this code, you're inserting into the DOM *eleven times*—once to insert the list and once for each list item. That's a huge amount. It would be better if you make the unordered list, but don't insert it into the DOM. You then add each list item to this unordered list and insert the entire thing into the DOM, taking your number of DOM insertions from eleven down to just one. That's really easy to do:

```
$(function() {
  var i = 0;
  var newUl = $("<ul />");
  while( i < 10 ) {
    $("<li />", {
      "text" : i+1
    }).appendTo(newUl);
    i++;
  }
  newUl.appendTo("body");
});
```

The key here is that you don't append the unordered list to the body until the loop is complete. You can create an element and add elements to it before you add that element to the DOM. That's the best way to do it. You're still appending each list item to the unordered list, but it's *not a DOM insertion* because that unordered list has not been added to the DOM. It's only added at the very end. While writing this, we were curious as to just how much difference that makes, and we found that doing the insertion within the loop was between *45 and 60 percent slower* than doing one insertion at the end. Granted, in this case, the difference is much less because you're only inserting ten elements, but you should always aim to produce efficient code, and watching out for situations like these is a large part of that.

Summary

In the space of one chapter, a vast amount was covered. Now that you can manipulate the DOM, you're capable of so much more than you were a chapter ago. Next up, you'll look at events and how to write code that's executed based on user interaction. You'll also build an accordion, putting together events and DOM manipulation.

CHAPTER 5

■ ■ ■

An Introduction to Events

When you write JavaScript in the browser, you're writing *event-driven* code. Most of your code will be executed when something happens, such as having content slide in when a user clicks a link. Even though you might not have realized it, you've already written some event-based code:

```
$(function() {
});
```

You've been writing code that runs when the document is ready, as previously explained. This is an event that you're attaching code to. It is also known as *binding*. Keeping the JavaScript in a separate document and binding it to the HTML document is good idea for a few reasons. The first is that it makes editing easier. Another reason is that it keeps people from injecting code into the HTML document and overriding your code.

So far you have bound some code to run on a certain event. In this chapter, you will look at the type of events and, at the end of the chapter, use your new knowledge to build an accordion. An *accordion* is a great way to include a lot of information in a small amount of room. It works by taking paragraphs of text—each under a heading—and showing only one section of text at a time. The user can navigate by clicking each heading to reveal the text below it. In the next chapter, you will delve further into events (it's a big subject) and improve what you learned in this chapter.

There are a lot of events in the browser that you can bind to. If you can think of an event, it's almost certain that you can bind to that event with jQuery. This chapter introduces the following events:

- `click`: Clicking an elements such as a button
- `hover`: Interacting with an element via the mouse; in pure JavaScript, known as `mouseenter` or `mouseleave`
- `submit`: Submitting a form
- `trigger`: Making an event happen
- `off`: Removing an event

The most popular is the `click` event.

A lot of older tutorials you'll see on the Web will tell you to use methods such as `click()` to bind code to a click event, like so:

```
$("div").click(function() {
  alert("clicked");
});
```

© Jack Franklin, Russ Ferguson 2017
J. Franklin, R. Ferguson, *Beginning jQuery*, https://doi.org/10.1007/978-1-4842-3027-5_5

This was the recommended way of doing it. However, there is an updated syntax for binding code to events.

■ **Note** Functions that are bound to an event are often referred to as *event handlers*.

Of course, the methods like click(), hover(), and so on all still work, but it's recommended to use the current API, which features primarily just one method—on()—to do the event binding for you.

The issue for people picking up jQuery is that the on() method can be pretty overwhelming, especially at the beginning. Because it does the job of a lot of other methods, it comes across as fairly complex. In practice though, it's not half as bad as you might think. Here's code to bind a click handler pre–jQuery 1.7 compared to the 1.7 way of doing things:

```
$("div").click(function() {
  alert("hello");
});

$("div").on("click", function() {
  alert("hello");
});
```

There's not much complexity here. Instead of using individual methods for all the different events, you pass the event name in as the first parameter and then the event handler in as the second.

Now for a quick history lesson. The reason for this change was simple: previously there were a huge number of methods, all focused on event binding. There were individual event handlers like click(), hover(), and so on. Then there were more methods for general event binding, such as bind(), live(), and delegate(). As you can imagine, this got complicated and required a lot of explaining. Those methods all still exist in jQuery, but it's highly advised that you switch to just using on(). That's the approach that we're taking in this book. on() is incredibly powerful, so much so that it will take this chapter and the next to fully cover everything you need to know about events.

Popular Events

Now that you know how to bind events, it's time to examine some of the ones I tend to use most often in day-to-day development. The most obvious is the click event, which you have already seen. This is the event you are likely going to use more than any other.

Another popular event is hover. Now, hover isn't actually an event, but it's shorthand for binding two functions at once—one to the mouseenter event, which is executed when the mouse hovers over the element in question, and one for the mouseleave event, which is when the mouse stops hovering over the element.

If you want to bind to a hover event, you can use the hover() method, which takes two functions:

```
$("div").hover(function() {
  alert("hovered in");
}, function() {
  alert("hovered out");
});
```

If you would rather use the new on() method, you have to use the mouseenter and mouseleave events:

```
$("div").on("mouseenter", function() {
  alert("hovered over");
}).on("mouseleave", function() {
  alert("hovered out");
});
```

By taking advantage of chaining, you can simply bind the mouseleave immediately after binding the mouseenter function.

However, there are multiple times when you will find yourself wanting to run code whenever the user hovers in or out. For example, often you might want to run some code to reset margins, stop animations, and so on. If this is the case, on() allows you to bind the same function to multiple events. Simply pass them into the on() method as a space-delimited string:

```
$("div").on("mouseenter mouseleave", function() {
  alert("hovered on or out");
});
```

You can bind to as many events as you want in one go:

```
$("div").on("mouseenter mouseleave click dblclick", function() {
  alert("hovered on or out, clicked or double clicked");
});
```

jQuery doesn't care how many events you bind to; it will do it. Obviously, this is impractical and there are not many times where you'd want to do this, but it's good to know. Sometimes you may want to run the same code on mouse on or mouse out, for example.

Binding multiple events presents a question: how do you know which event triggered the function? It's a good question—and one we'll answer shortly in this chapter.

Back to the subject of events, you might have noticed that the previous binding example just introduced another event: double-click, which is named dblclick. That wraps up the important mouse events that you need to know, for now. The next chapter will go over a few that we are skipping for the moment. As a recap, the main mouse events you need to be aware of are:

- click
- mouseenter
- mouseleave
- dblclick

Another important part of jQuery's events are the form events. jQuery makes enhancing forms using JavaScript—such as custom validation—really straightforward. For additional security, it is also important to have validation on the server side. JavaScript can help with making sure an e-mail address is formatted correctly, but it does not know what is happing in your database.

A large part of jQuery's simplicity comes down to the events you're able to hook into. The main one is submit, which is fired when a form is submitted. You don't have to bind this event to the Submit button on a form, but *to the form itself*. For example, with this HTML:

```
<form action="/some/url" method="get">
  <label>Enter your first name: </label>
  <input type="text" name="first_name" >
  <input type="submit" name="submit" value="Submit">
</form>
```

you could run code when the form is submitted just by binding to the submit element on the form:

```
$("form").on("submit", function() {
  alert("you just submitted the form!");
});
```

For dealing with events on individual inputs, the two events you will use most often are focus and blur, which are exact opposites of each other. The focus event is fired when an element has focus. The most obvious example is when the user clicks an input box or starts typing in it. At that moment, the element has focus and the focus event is fired. When the user moves on, clicking another element or just off that element, the blur method is fired. Think of focus and blur as being a little like mouseenter and mouseleave in how they work. The most important difference is that focus and blur can be triggered in more ways than just via a mouse. They can also be triggered via the keyboard when the user tabs through a form. Thus, for events to be fired based on an input element being active, never use mouseenter or mouseleave. Always use focus and blur.

```
$("input").on("focus", function() {
  alert("you're focused on an input");
}).on("blur", function() {
  alert("this input just lost focus");
});
```

Interacting with the Element

When an element fires an event, one of the things you'll frequently need to do is perform actions with the element that's been interacted with. Perhaps you want to hide it when it's clicked, or slowly fade it in or out. Within the event handler, you have access to the current element through the this keyword. You've already seen the this keyword previously in your animation callbacks, and it works the same way for events. When the event is fired, the this keyword is bound to the element that fired the event.

Be aware, the this keyword is *not* set to a jQuery object with the element in, but only to the DOM element reference. To get a jQuery reference, simply pass it into the jQuery object:

```
$("div").on("click", function() {
  alert($(this).attr("class"));
});
```

If you're going to reference the element multiple times, it's best to get a jQuery reference to it and then save that to a variable:

```
$("div").on("click", function() {
  var t = $(this);
  alert(t.attr("class"));
});
```

In this case we are calling the variable t, but there are a few different conventions. A lot of people will go for the variable name that; others go for $this, $t, or self. It doesn't matter what you call it really—just make sure that it's sensible and consistent. There's nothing worse than coming back to your code to see you've used different variable names in different places!

Triggering Events

Sometimes you might want to manually trigger an event. Perhaps you've got a link that enables the user to fill out a form, and when it's clicked you'd like to fire the submit event on a form. jQuery has the `trigger()` method to do this for us:

```
$("a").on("click", function() {
  $("form").trigger("submit");
});
```

This can be useful in certain situations; however, if you find yourself doing it frequently, there's a chance you might want to rethink your code. You shouldn't be continuously triggering artificial events, but there may be times when it's useful. For example, if you are working on some code that allows the user to click links to navigate through a set of images, it's a good idea to make that work with the arrow buttons on a keyboard, too. Thus, you might want the navigational link to have a click event triggered when you detect that the arrow keys have been clicked.

Unbinding from Events

Just as you have on() for binding to events, you have off() for unbinding from events. In its simplest form, it's used like so:

```
$("div").off();
```

That will unbind all events from every div. You can also pass in an event as the first parameter to unbind all events of that type. The following code unbinds all click events from paragraphs, so clicking a paragraph does nothing:

```
$("p").on("click", function() {
  alert("click " + this.id);
});

$("p").off("click");
```

It's also possible to unbind just a specific function. Looking at the following code, see if you can figure out what will happen when you click a paragraph:

```
$(function() {
  var clickEvent = function() {
    alert("clickEvent");
  };
  $("p").on("click", function() {
    alert("click");
  }).on("click", clickEvent);

  $("p").off("click", clickEvent);
});
```

Which one of the following do you think will happen?

- You get two alerts: one saying "clickEvent" and the other saying "click"
- You get just one alert saying "click"
- You get just one alert saying "clickEvent"

If you guessed the middle option, you're correct. When you bind the function stored in the variable clickEvent to the event, you can unbind only that function by passing it, along with an event type, into the off() method.

You won't find yourself using the off() method too frequently, but as with a lot of the things you've seen so far in this chapter, there are places where it comes in handy. Maybe you only want to allow a button to be clicked a certain number of times, in which case you would keep count of the number of clicks and use off() when the counter reaches the maximum that you want to allow.

The Event Object

Earlier we said that binding multiple events presents a question: How do you know which event triggered the function? And now you're going to find out the answer.

Whenever you bind an event to a function and that function is then triggered, jQuery passes what's known as the *event object*. This object contains a lot of information about the event. To get access to this, just make your event handler take one parameter as an argument. jQuery then passes the event object into this function, and you can get at it through the argument that you denoted your function should take. For example:

```
$(function() {
        $("p").on("click", function(event) {
          console.log(event);
        });
      });
```

As you've seen, you don't have to do this. If you've no interest in the event object, don't add the argument. JavaScript doesn't give an error if you pass a function an argument that it doesn't accept. The event object contains a lot of properties. The results will be the same in all browsers. Here's the output when logging it to the Google Chrome console:

```
altKey: false
attrChange: undefined
attrName: undefined
bubbles: true
button: 0
buttons: undefined
cancelable: true
clientX: 21
clientY: 54
ctrlKey: false
currentTarget: HTMLParagraphElement
data: undefined
delegateTarget: HTMLParagraphElement
eventPhase: 2
fromElement: null
```

```
handleObj: Object
isDefaultPrevented: function ba(){return!1}
jQuery18008258051469456404: true
metaKey: false
offsetX: 13
offsetY: 4
originalEvent: MouseEvent
pageX: 21
pageY: 54
relatedNode: undefined
relatedTarget: null
screenX: 21
screenY: 148
shiftKey: false
srcElement: HTMLParagraphElement
target: HTMLParagraphElement
timeStamp: 1348853095547
toElement: HTMLParagraphElement
type: "click"
view: Window
which: 1
```

There's an awful lot of stuff there—a lot of which you won't ever care about most of the time. In the following code, we've picked out a few key attributes that are worth knowing. A few of these attributes you will use, but not until a bit later in the book.

Remember the question posed earlier about how to find out which event was fired? The event object contains a type property, which does just this. This is useful for binding a function to the hover event:

```
$(function() {
  $("div").on("hover", function(event) {
    if(event.type === "mouseenter") {
      $(this).css("background", "blue");
    } else {
      $(this).css("background", "red");
    }
  });
});
```

You know that when you bind to "hover", it will fire on mouseenter or mouseleave ("hover" is just a handy shortcut that jQuery provides), so all you have to do is a simple statement within the event handler to determine the type. The preceding code will make the div turn blue when you hover your mouse over it and red when you leave it.

You can use the pageX and pageY properties to get the position of the mouse when the event fired, *relative to the top-left edge of the document window.*

```
$(function() {
  $("div").on("click", function(event) {
    alert("Your mouse is at X " + event.pageX + " and at Y " + event.pageY);
  });
});
```

This will bring up an alert box whenever the link is clicked, showing the coordinates of the mouse pointer, as shown in Figure 5-1.

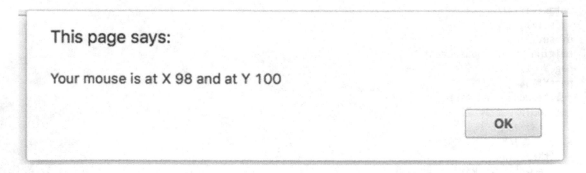

This page says:

Your mouse is at X 98 and at Y 100

OK

Figure 5-1. *The alert box showing the position of the mouse pointer when the link is clicked*

We'll cover more of these properties in greater detail later. For now, it's time to build something!

Building an Accordion

Up until now, the code that we've asked you to write has been small and typically used to show a small feature. This time, you're going to pull together what you've learned in the past few chapters and build a basic accordion. Once you study events in further details in the next chapter, you will visit this code again and improve it.

Start a new project and create the usual structure, an index.html file containing nothing but

```
<!DOCTYPE html>
<html>
  <head>
    <title>Chapter 05, Accordion</title>
    <script src="jquery.js"></script>
    <script src="app.js"></script>
    <link rel="stylesheet" href="style.css" />
  </head>
  <body>
  </body>
</html>
```

Include the jQuery source and an app.js file that simply contains

```
$(function() {
});
```

You'll also need to do a bit of basic CSS styling, so add a blank style.css.

You're going to use a basic HTML structure of headings and paragraphs, contained within a `div`:

```
<div id="accordion">
<h2>Heading</h2>
<p>Lorem ipsum dolor sit amet, consectetur adipisicing elit, sed do eiusmod tempor
incididunt ut labore et dolore magna aliqua. Ut enim ad minim veniam, quis nostrud
exercitation ullamco laboris nisi ut aliquip ex ea commodo consequat. Duis aute irure dolor
in reprehenderit in voluptate velit esse cillum dolore eu fugiat nulla pariatur. Excepteur
sint occaecat cupidatat non proident, sunt in culpa qui officia deserunt mollit anim id est
laborum.</p>
<h2>Heading 2</h2>
<p>Lorem ipsum dolor sit amet, consectetur adipisicing elit, sed do eiusmod tempor
incididunt ut labore et dolore magna aliqua. Ut enim ad minim veniam, quis nostrud
exercitation ullamco laboris nisi ut aliquip ex ea commodo consequat. Duis aute irure dolor
in reprehenderit in voluptate velit esse cillum dolore eu fugiat nulla pariatur. Excepteur
sint occaecat cupidatat non proident, sunt in culpa qui officia deserunt mollit anim id est
laborum.</p>
<h2>Heading 3</h2>
<p>Lorem ipsum dolor sit amet, consectetur adipisicing elit, sed do eiusmod tempor
incididunt ut labore et dolore magna aliqua. Ut enim ad minim veniam, quis nostrud
exercitation ullamco laboris nisi ut aliquip ex ea commodo consequat. Duis aute irure dolor
in reprehenderit in voluptate velit esse cillum dolore eu fugiat nulla pariatur. Excepteur
sint occaecat cupidatat non proident, sunt in culpa qui officia deserunt mollit anim id est
laborum.</p>
</div>
```

The first thing you need to do is style your accordion. This isn't a book on CSS, so the details aren't important, but all you're doing here is adding structure to the HTML with some simple rules:

```
#accordion {
  width: 500px;
  border: 1px solid black;
}

#accordion h2 {
  padding: 5px;
  margin: 0;
  background: #ddd;
}

#accordion p {
  padding: 0 5px;
}
```

This leaves you with the image shown in Figure 5-2.

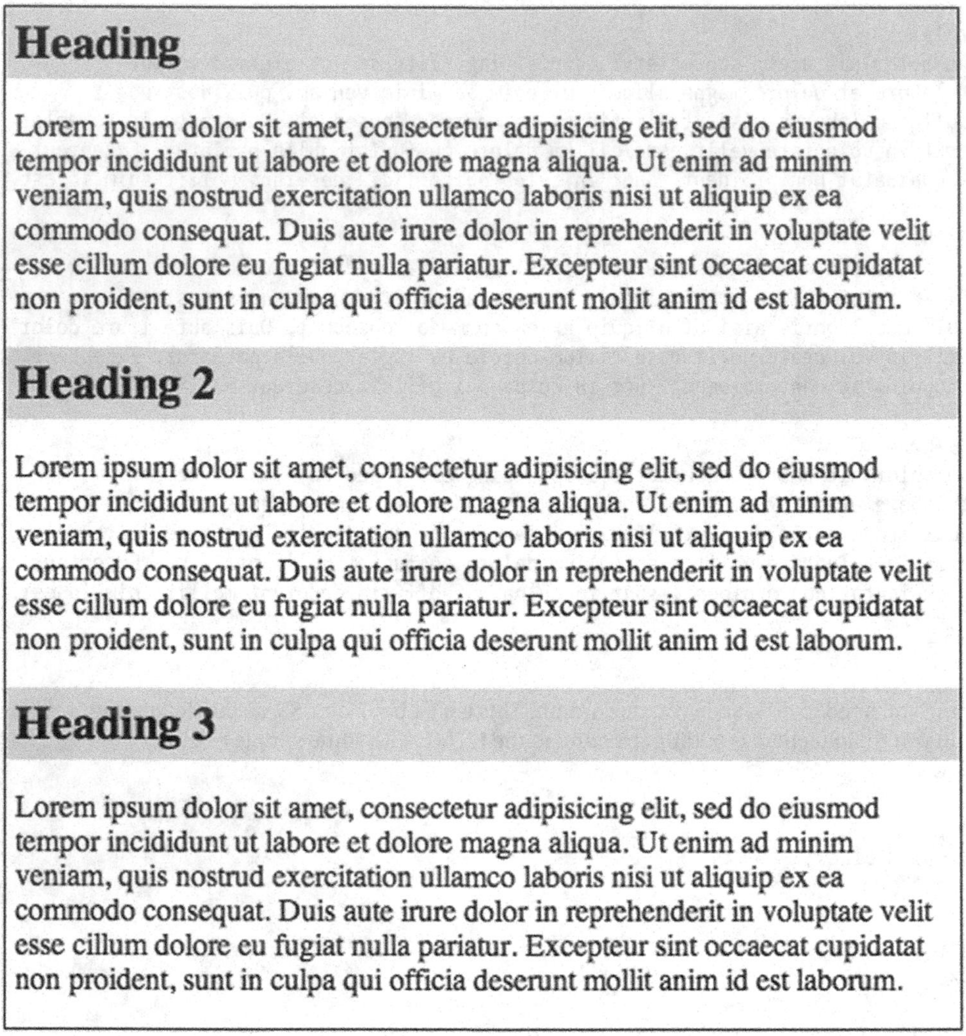

Heading

Lorem ipsum dolor sit amet, consectetur adipisicing elit, sed do eiusmod tempor incididunt ut labore et dolore magna aliqua. Ut enim ad minim veniam, quis nostrud exercitation ullamco laboris nisi ut aliquip ex ea commodo consequat. Duis aute irure dolor in reprehenderit in voluptate velit esse cillum dolore eu fugiat nulla pariatur. Excepteur sint occaecat cupidatat non proident, sunt in culpa qui officia deserunt mollit anim id est laborum.

Heading 2

Lorem ipsum dolor sit amet, consectetur adipisicing elit, sed do eiusmod tempor incididunt ut labore et dolore magna aliqua. Ut enim ad minim veniam, quis nostrud exercitation ullamco laboris nisi ut aliquip ex ea commodo consequat. Duis aute irure dolor in reprehenderit in voluptate velit esse cillum dolore eu fugiat nulla pariatur. Excepteur sint occaecat cupidatat non proident, sunt in culpa qui officia deserunt mollit anim id est laborum.

Heading 3

Lorem ipsum dolor sit amet, consectetur adipisicing elit, sed do eiusmod tempor incididunt ut labore et dolore magna aliqua. Ut enim ad minim veniam, quis nostrud exercitation ullamco laboris nisi ut aliquip ex ea commodo consequat. Duis aute irure dolor in reprehenderit in voluptate velit esse cillum dolore eu fugiat nulla pariatur. Excepteur sint occaecat cupidatat non proident, sunt in culpa qui officia deserunt mollit anim id est laborum.

Figure 5-2. *The basic accordion structure, before any JavaScript has been applied*

Now you need to hide all the paragraphs except for the first. This could be done with CSS, but when working on anything like this, you need to make sure the content is still accessible with JavaScript turned off. Thus, you hide the content with JavaScript, so if a user does not have it enabled, he or she can still see the content.

Head over to `app.js`, which at this point should just contain the code that binds a function to the `ready` event. The first thing to do is the initial setup, so get all the headers and paragraphs stored in variables:

```
var headings = $("h2");
var paragraphs = $("p");
```

Now you want to hide all but the first paragraph. Chapter 4 discussed traversing the DOM, and one of the methods briefly mentioned was not(), a filter method. You can use this to filter your selection down to all but the first paragraph, and hide the rest:

```
$(function() {
  var headings = $("h2");
  var paragraphs = $("p");
  paragraphs.not(":first").hide();
});
```

If you look in the browser, you should see what's shown in Figure 5-3.

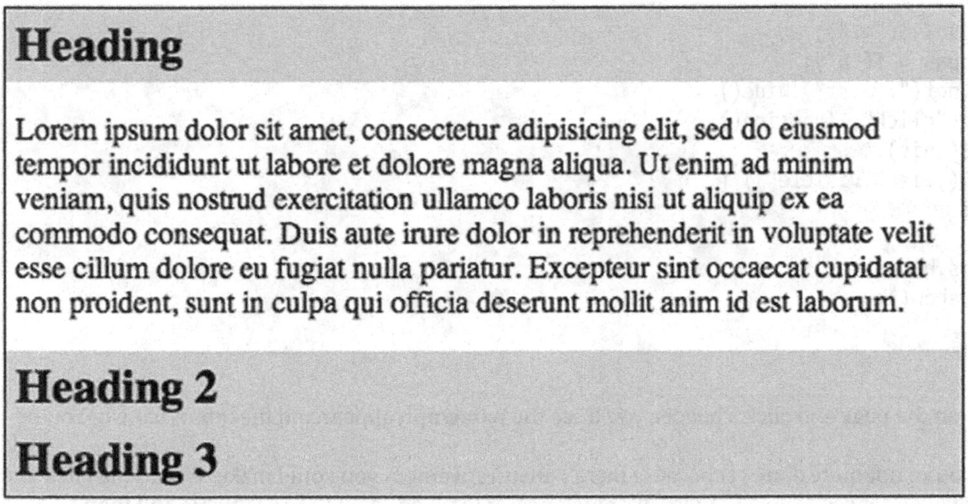

Heading

Lorem ipsum dolor sit amet, consectetur adipisicing elit, sed do eiusmod tempor incididunt ut labore et dolore magna aliqua. Ut enim ad minim veniam, quis nostrud exercitation ullamco laboris nisi ut aliquip ex ea commodo consequat. Duis aute irure dolor in reprehenderit in voluptate velit esse cillum dolore eu fugiat nulla pariatur. Excepteur sint occaecat cupidatat non proident, sunt in culpa qui officia deserunt mollit anim id est laborum.

Heading 2

Heading 3

Figure 5-3. *The accordion, with only one section showing*

Now you can work on the code to run when a header is clicked. You need to do the following:

- Hide the currently visible paragraph.
- Show the paragraph that's immediately after the header that was clicked.

But you should only do this if the header isn't the currently active header—else you'd be hiding and showing the same paragraph.

When a header is clicked, the first thing to do is check whether the paragraph underneath it is visible. If it is, then you don't need to do anything. That's established like so:

```
headings.on("click", function() {
  var t = $(this);
  if(t.next().is(":visible")) {
    return;
  }
});
```

After binding the click handler and storing the value of $(this) in the variable t, you then need a way to access the paragraph. Chapter 4 covered the next() method. It is used to get the element that immediately follows the current one in the DOM. Based on your HTML, this will always be the relevant paragraph to the header that was clicked. You then need to use the is() method. It is passed a selector, in this case ":visible", and will return true if the element matches the selector, and false if it does not.

If it does match the selector, it means that it's visible, so all you do is return. Using the return keyword causes the function to stop execution at that point, and no further code in that function will be run. This is a great way to stop running the code if you're running it on an element that you don't need to.

If t.next().is(":visible") returns false, you know that you need to show that paragraph and hide the others. Rather than specifically hide the visible paragraph, in this instance it's much easier to hide them all, and then show only the one you need:

```
$(function() {
  var headings = $("h2");
  var paragraphs = $("p");
  paragraphs.not(":first").hide();
  headings.on("click", function() {
    var t = $(this);
    if(t.next().is(":visible")) {
      return;
    }
    paragraphs.hide();
    t.next().show();
  });
});
```

If you refresh the page and click a header, you'll see the paragraph appear and the others vanish. You're done!

Actually, you're not quite done yet because there's an improvement you could make. Within the click handler, you have referenced t.next() twice. It's much neater to save t.next() to a variable and then reference that:

```
$(function() {
  var headings = $("h2");
  var paragraphs = $("p");
  paragraphs.not(":first").hide();
  headings.on("click", function() {
    var t = $(this);
    var tPara = t.next();
    if(tPara.is(":visible")) {
      return;
    }
    paragraphs.hide();
    tPara.show();
  });
});
```

Also, it would be nice if you had some animation here, so make the paragraphs slide in and out of view, rather than just appearing and hiding instantly. This is really straightforward—simply change the last two lines within the event handler:

```
$(function() {
  var headings = $("h2");
  var paragraphs = $("p");
  paragraphs.not(":first").hide();
  headings.on("click", function() {
    var t = $(this);
    var tPara = t.next();
    if(tPara.is(":visible")) {
      return;
    }
    paragraphs.slideUp("normal");
    tPara.slideDown("normal");
  });
});
```

Now you should get some nicely animated paragraphs as you click the headers. Congratulations, you've just built your first jQuery accordion!

Summary

That accordion isn't perfect, as you'll soon discover in the next chapter. Events are such an important part of jQuery (and JavaScript) development that we've dedicated two chapters to them. In the next chapter, you'll look at some of the issues in your accordion. You'll also take a closer look at events—including some skipped over in this chapter—and rewrite your accordion to make it much more foolproof.

CHAPTER 6

■ ■ ■

More Events

At the end of the last chapter, you ended up with a respectable accordion, which was the first major bit of jQuery you'd embarked on. You might not have realized it, but the code you wrote could be tidied up. In this chapter, you'll round out your knowledge of events by looking at the more advanced features, including:

- Event delegation
- Event propagation
- Preventing default behavior
- Creating your own events

Once you've covered these features, you'll take another look at your accordion and do some refactoring to improve the code and make it more efficient. Chapter 7 will look at animation in depth, and you'll again use the accordion example to improve the animations in it. But first, it's time to dive into event delegation.

Event Delegation

Imagine that you have 100 paragraphs on a page and you want something to happen every time a user clicks one of them. Knowing what you do about jQuery, you would probably, quite reasonably, write something like this:

```
$("p").on("click", function() {
  //do something here
});
```

And this would work fine, but it is terribly inefficient. Why? This code makes the browser loop over every single paragraph individually and bind an event handler to it. That means it has to bind 100 individual event handlers 100 times to 100 individual paragraphs. When you're writing code and you notice that a browser has to do something multiple times in quick succession, it's time to start thinking about whether there's a nicer way to write the code to avoid it.

There's also another problem with this code. Imagine that the user can add new content on your page, which is then saved to your system through some back-end system. This means the user might be adding new paragraphs to the page, and you still want the event handler that you bound earlier to work on these newly inserted paragraphs. In the following code, if you insert a new paragraph to the DOM and click it, will you see the alert box?

```
$("p").on("click", function() {
  alert("Hello World");
});
// insert new paragraph code here
```

© Jack Franklin, Russ Ferguson 2017
J. Franklin, R. Ferguson, *Beginning jQuery*, https://doi.org/10.1007/978-1-4842-3027-5_6

The answer is no, clicking the new paragraph will not show the alert. Consider why this might be.

When you run $("p"), it selects all current paragraph elements on the page. This is not a "live" selector that updates whenever you insert new content. It selects elements in the DOM *at the time* but *does not* update itself. So there are now have two problems to solve:

1. How can you run a function whenever a paragraph is clicked, but still bind it efficiently when there are a lot of paragraphs?

2. How can you make it so any new paragraphs inserted into the DOM also run the code when they are clicked?

The answer, as you might have guessed, is *event delegation.* It means that instead of binding the event to each paragraph individually, you bind the event to a parent element of all the paragraphs and let it *delegate* the event to the paragraph. This sounds more complicated than it is. Here's an explanation of how it works:

- The click event is bound to a parent element of all your paragraphs (keep it simple and use the body element for this example).

- When the body element detects an event of the type you bound (click, in this case), it checks to see if the click happened on a paragraph.

- If the click happened, the body element fires. This is where the delegation happens.

The major advantage of binding this way is that you have to bind *one handler* to *one element* and do it just once. That's a lot better than doing it 100 times over, as you did previously. And because this event is bound to a parent element, and not to the paragraphs, this will work for any new paragraphs you insert!

Let's look at how you do this in practice. As always, set up an index.html file that includes jQuery and a blank app.js. You can add some styling if you like, but that's optional. Within the body, add paragraphs.

```html
<!DOCTYPE html>
<html>
  <head>
    <title>Chapter 06, Exercise 01</title>
    <script src="jquery.js"></script>
    <script src="app.js"></script>
  </head>
  <body>
    <p>Paragraph 1</p>
    <p>Paragraph 2</p>
    <p>Paragraph 3</p>
    <p>Paragraph 4</p>
    <p>Paragraph 5</p>
  </body>
</html>
```

Head into app.js and add this:

```javascript
$(function() {
  $("p").on("click", function() {
    alert("Hello World");
  });
  $("<p />", {
    text: "Paragraph 6"
  }).appendTo("body");
});
```

Notice how you bind the click event as you did in the previous chapter, and then insert a new paragraph. If you open index.html in a browser and click the paragraphs, you'll see that the first five (the ones that existed initially) all give you the alert, but clicking the sixth (the paragraph you inserted after binding the click event) doesn't give you the alert. Use event delegation to fix that. The change is brilliantly simple:

```
$(function() {
  $("body").on("click", "p", function() {
    alert("Hello World");
  });
  $("<p />", {
    text: "Paragraph 6"
  }).appendTo("body");
});
```

The key (and in fact, only) change is this line:

```
$("body").on("click", "p", function() {...});
```

Previously, when you used the on() method, you used it in the form:

```
$(selector).on(event, function() {...});
```

When used in this form, the event is bound to the selector; however, you can also use it in this form:

```
$(selector).on(event, delegateSelector, function() {...});
```

When it is used in this form, the event is still bound to the selector, but it will delegate it to any elements that match the delegateSelector that are children of it. If you make that change and refresh the page in the browser, clicking the sixth paragraph will work as desired and display the alert. What you're doing is binding the click event to the body and telling it to delegate it to all paragraphs within it. This means it doesn't care when the paragraph first existed—as long as it's within the body and is clicked, the event will fire.

You shouldn't go over the top when it comes to deciding when to delegate. The key rule here is common sense: if you're binding an event to just one element, there's no point in delegating because you don't gain anything. The rule we recommend is not to delegate when you're binding to more than a few elements, perhaps anything over five. In reality, it's not going to matter much if you don't delegate. The performance gains are minimal for a small number of links, but it's still something you should do. Even if the optimizations you make are small, they are still worth making.

Event Propagation

Event propagation is something that can cause people new to JavaScript events a bit of trouble, so it's best explained with an example before diving into it. Imagine that you have a div, and within that div, there's a heading. You want to run one piece of code when the div is clicked, and another when the heading is clicked. Easy, right? Take a look. As always, you've got your index.html:

```
<!DOCTYPE html>
<html>
  <head>
    <title>Chapter 06, Exercise 02</title>
    <script src="jquery.js"></script>
```

```
    <script src="app.js"></script>
    <link rel="stylesheet" href="style.css" />
  </head>
  <body>
    <div>
      <h5>Hello</h5>
    </div>
  </body>
</html>
```

Here's your app.js:

```
$(function() {
});
```

Also include the jQuery source in index.html and add a quick bit of CSS in style.css to style things so that it's easier to see what's going on:

```
div {
  width: 500px;
  height: 500px;
  background: red;
  padding: 20px;
}

h5 {
  border: 1px solid black;
  background: white;
  width: 300px;
  font-size: 20px;
  top: 20px;
}
```

This would produce a result like the one shown in Figure 6-1.

Figure 6-1. The results of the CSS styling

This gives you a very basic page. Now write the code to alert a message when you click the header, and alert a different message when you click the div:

```
$(function() {
  $("h5").on("click", function() {
    alert("header");
  });
  $("div").on("click", function() {
    alert("div");
  });
});
```

Refresh your browser and click the div. You'll see the correct alert, "div". Now click the header. You will see two alerts pop up—one with the text "header" and the other with "div". What just happened there? You guessed it: you just saw *event propagation* in action.

You may have heard of the phrase *event bubbling*. Event propagation is the same as event bubbling; they are simply two terms meaning the same thing.

When an event is fired on an element in the browser, it's not just fired on that element, but every element that is a parent of it. When you click the heading in your example, you also click the div. The heading is within the div, which means you didn't just click the heading, but the div, too. You also registered a click event on the parent of the div, which in this case is the body. That's why you get two alert boxes when you click the heading—because you've also clicked the div. While most events (including the ones you'll work with most often) propagate, not all of them do. The Wikipedia page on DOM events (https://en.wikipedia.org/wiki/DOM_events) has a handy table showing all DOM events and whether they propagate.

When Should I Worry About Event Propagation?

Typically, the only time you need to worry about event propagation is when you are binding an event to both an element and the element's parent. Most of the time, event propagation is something you won't have to worry about—demonstrated by the fact that it was not mentioned in the first five chapters of the book. If it caused the average developer more issues, it would have come up much earlier.

Luckily, there is a way to stop event propagation. You'll recall that earlier you learned information about an event by passing an event object into your event handler functions, like so:

```
$("div").on("click", function(event) {...});
```

While the event object contains a lot of information about the event, it also contains methods that you can use. One of those methods is stopPropagation(). Here's what the jQuery API (http://api.jquery.com/event.stopPropagation/) has to say about it: "Prevents the event from bubbling up the DOM tree, preventing any parent handlers from being notified of the event."

Therefore, you can pass in an event object, call stopPropagation(), and solve the issue you have with your code. Look at the change required:

```
$(function() {
  $("h5").on("click", function(event) {
    alert("header");
    event.stopPropagation();
  });
  $("div").on("click", function() {
    alert("div");
  });
});
```

When you click the header now, you will only see one alert that contains the text "header", as desired.

Just because you can do something, doesn't mean you should—and that rings true with preventing propagation. Unless the propagation of an event is causing an issue, don't prevent it. In practice, propagation rarely causes any problems.

Preventing Default Behavior

Sometimes when you bind to an event, you need to stop the browser from performing the default action attached to that event. For example, when an anchor element is clicked, the default browser behavior is to follow that link. Sometimes you're going to want to override this. Perhaps you want the link to appear in a pop-up window, so decide to bind to the event and implement your pop-up code. Let's see how you might do this. Here's an index.html file with a link in it:

```
<!DOCTYPE html>
<html>
  <head>
    <title>Chapter 06, Exercise 04</title>
    <script src="jquery.js"></script>
    <script src="app.js"></script>
    <link rel="stylesheet" href="style.css" />
  </head>
  <body>
    <div>
      <a href="http://www.apress.com">Apress</a>
    </div>
  </body>
</html>
```

That link is within a div, and as a simplified example, suppose that when the link is clicked, you'd like the background of the div to change to blue, and then nothing more to happen. The first attempt at this would probably look like so:

```
$(function() {
  $("a").on("click", function() {
    $("div").css("background", "blue");
  });
});
```

If you try that in your browser, you will see the div turn blue for a split second before you are taken to the Apress web site. So, while it is executing your code, it's then immediately whisking the user off to another site, rendering your code useless.

On the event object, along with stopPropagation(), there's also preventDefault(), and you can probably figure out what that one does. You use it just as you did with stopPropagation()—pass in an event object to the event handler and then call preventDefault() on that object:

```
$(function() {
  $("a").on("click", function(event) {
    event.preventDefault();
    $("div").css("background", "blue");
  });
});
```

It's important to note that it does not matter where in the event handler you call preventDefault() (and the same goes for stopPropagation()). Some people like to call it at the end, some at the beginning, and some in the middle. Usually it is put and the end, and we can explain why.

If you call preventDefault() at the very start of the event handler, it immediately prevents the browser's default action from occurring. If some other code in the event handler causes an error, two things have happened:

- The default browser event didn't fire because you called preventDefault() on the very first line.

- The JavaScript you bound to the event didn't fire because there was an error.

Now imagine that you had the call to preventDefault() at the end, and some of your JavaScript in the event handler function errored.

- Your JavaScript wouldn't fire because there was an error.

- That error would mean that preventDefault() *wasn't* called, so the browser's default behavior would happen.

Having the browser's default behavior happen when your JavaScript errors is usually a good thing—it doesn't leave the user's browser totally broken (or at least, it won't seem that way to them).

A Note on return false;

In a lot of tutorials, you will see the use of return false; in handlers:

```
$(function() {
  $("a").on("click", function() {
    $("div").css("background", "blue");
    return false;
  });
});
```

Making a handler return Boolean false has the effect of stopping the default event action from being called and stopping the event from propagating. In essence, it effectively is a shortcut for calling stopPropagation() and preventDefault(). As previously explained, most of the time you actually don't want to call stopPropagation(), so we strongly advise avoiding return false, and instead use preventDefault().

Your Own Events

A seldom-used but very useful feature of jQuery's events is the ability to trigger and bind to your own custom events. You might be reading this thinking, "Why?". This section explains why you would want to use this feature.

When you have a complex web site with multiple events firing, your code can get a bit messy. Suppose that when the user clicked a button, you had to perform a few distinct actions. Perhaps you had to update the title, change the background color, and a few other things. You could add all of these within the one event handler for the click event for this button, but soon things will get messy. And then you realize that one of these bits of functionality—perhaps changing the background color—needs to happen either when the user clicks the button or hovers over a certain element. From here, your code is going to get messy, quickly. You can't copy and paste the same code into two different event handlers because that would be sloppy. You could pull the code into a function, which wouldn't be too bad. Or, you could create a custom event—and have the best of both worlds. If you're still not convinced, just hold tight and hopefully the following example will win you over.

As always, create a new folder for this example, which has an `index.html`:

```html
<!DOCTYPE html>
<html>
  <head>
    <title>Chapter 06, Exercise 05</title>
    <script src="jquery.js"></script>
    <script src="app.js"></script>
    <link rel="stylesheet" type="text/css" href="style.css" />
  </head>
  <body>
    <div>
      <h5>Click Me</h5>
      <h5>Or Me</h5>
    </div>
  </body>
</html>
```

Create an empty `app.js` file and a style sheet to which you can add basic styling:

```css
div {
  width: 500px;
  height: 500px;
  background-color: red;
  padding: 20px;
}

h5 {
  border: 1px solid black;
  background: white;
  width: 300px;
  font-size: 20px;
  top: 20px;
}
```

It's also got a local copy of the jQuery source. After that quick bit of CSS styling, you end up with your page looking like what's shown in Figure 6-2.

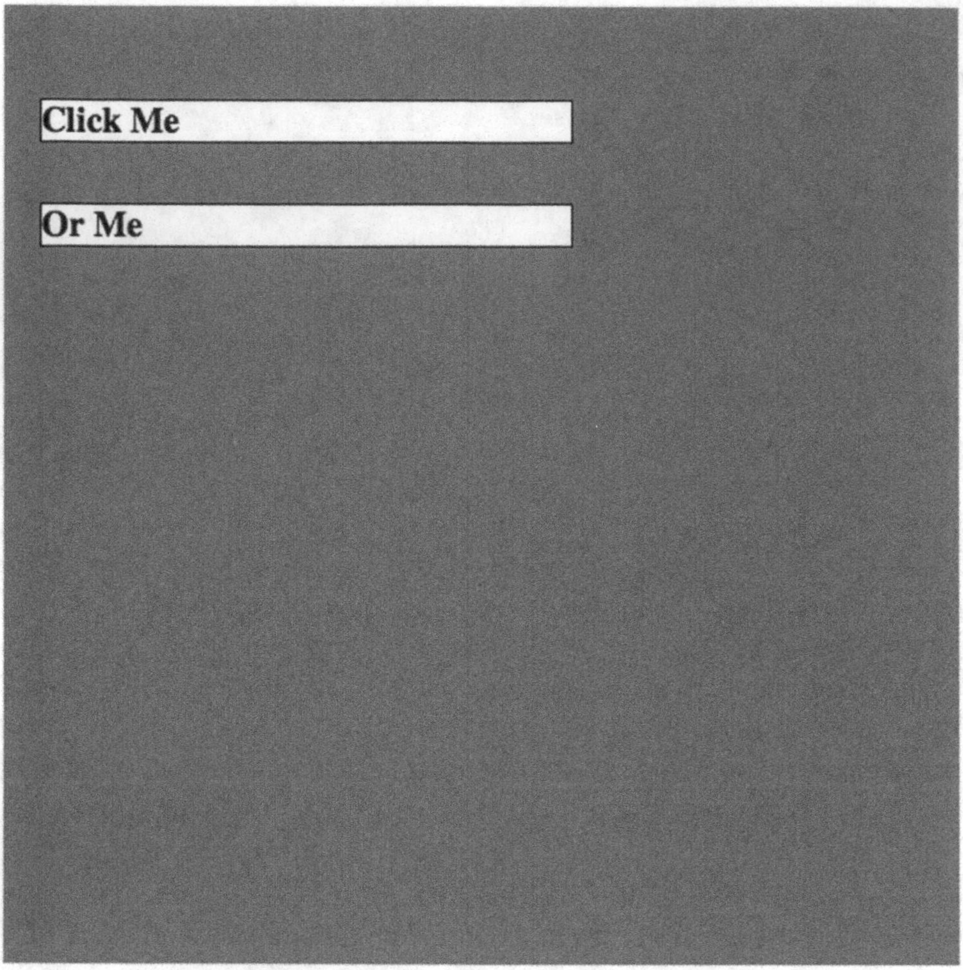

Figure 6-2. *The page with some basic CSS styling*

Now imagine that you need to change the background color of the div whenever either of those headers is clicked. The following triggers a custom event when those headers are clicked:

```
$(function() {
  $("h5").on("click", function() {
    $("div").trigger("bgchange");
  });
});
```

An event has to be triggered on an element, so this triggers it on the div. Now you can bind a function to that event just as you would for any other event:

```
$(function() {
  $("h5").on("click", function() {
    $("div").trigger("bgchange");
  });
```

86

```
$("div").on("bgchange", function() {
  var t = $(this);
  t.css("background-color", "blue");
});
});
```

The beauty of custom events is that they give you a neat way to package up your code and keep as much of it separate as possible. If your code can be purely *event driven*, that's a good thing. Rather than having lots of code interacting with other functions, simply trigger and bind to custom events. It will make your life easier. It also allows you to assign meaningful names to the events you create, keeping your code easy to follow and maintain.

The Accordion, Take 2

Building on the knowledge covered in this chapter, it's time to revisit the JavaScript you wrote for the accordion and see if you can improve it. Here it is again:

```
$(function() {
  var headings = $("h2");
  var paragraphs = $("p");
  paragraphs.not(":first").hide();
  headings.on("click", function() {
    var t = $(this);
    var tPara = t.next();
    if(tPara.is(":visible")) {
      return;
    }
    paragraphs.slideUp("normal");
    tPara.slideDown("normal");
  });
});
```

Seeing as this accordion could grow into many more headings than the three you have right now, switch from binding directly to the click event on the heading to delegating:

```
$(function() {
  var accordion = $("#accordion");
  var headings = $("h2");
  var paragraphs = $("p");
  paragraphs.not(":first").hide();
  accordion.on("click", "h2", function() {
    var t = $(this);
    var tPara = t.next();
    if(tPara.is(":visible")) {
      return;
    }
    paragraphs.slideUp("normal");
    tPara.slideDown("normal");
  });
});
```

Note the line added to save the accordion to a variable. Although you only reference it once, it's something you could easily find yourself referencing again, so there's not much harm done in saving it to a variable. You then switch the line that binds the event to use the delegation syntax covered in this chapter.

That still works great, but clicking the header might not be the only way to show a particular paragraph. Next, you're going to make the paragraphs slide down when a custom event is triggered on them, and then make clicking the header trigger that event.

Write the code that will make the paragraph slide down when it detects the event:

```
accordion.on("showParagraph", "p", function() {
  paragraphs.slideUp("normal");
  $(this).slideDown("normal");
});
```

Again, you use delegation for this, just as you did with the headings. Remember, custom events are handled just like regular events.

You can then rewrite the event handler for clicking the headings like so:

```
accordion.on("click", "h2", function() {
  var t = $(this);
  var tPara = t.next();
  if(!tPara.is(":visible")) {
    tPara.trigger("showParagraph");
  }
});
```

You'll notice this is now far simpler and easier to read. Within the click handler, check to see if !tPara.is(":visible") is true (note the exclamation mark at the beginning), and if it is, you then trigger the showParagraph event on the paragraph that you need to show. That leaves your entire code looking like the following:

```
$(function() {
  var accordion = $("#accordion");
  var headings = $("h2");
  var paragraphs = $("p");
  paragraphs.not(":first").hide();
  accordion.on("click", "h2", function() {
    var t = $(this);
    var tPara = t.next();
    if(!tPara.is(":visible")) {
      tPara.trigger("showParagraph");
    }
  });

  accordion.on("showParagraph", "p", function() {
    paragraphs.slideUp("normal");
    $(this).slideDown("normal");
  });
});
```

This might not seem easier. In fact, your code is a bit easier, but it's also more efficient, thanks to delegation, and it is easy to add other ways to trigger the correct paragraph sliding down. If you wanted to trigger a paragraph sliding down from another method, all you have to do is trigger the event on it. It's simple and extensible.

Summary

You should be pretty comfortable handling events in jQuery. This is good because they are used constantly in any jQuery project, both in this book and in real life. Your accordion is now much nicer and you are able to prevent default behavior, you have a good understanding of event propagation, and you can even trigger your own events. The accordion is now better for it.

It's still not perfect, however. In Chapter 7, you will dive further into animation, which will highlight some problems with the accordion as it stands. You'll also explore the more complex areas of animation and, at the end of the chapter, revisit the accordion to improve it.

CHAPTER 7

■■■

Animation

The subject of animation has been broached multiple times in this book so far, but only the very basic bits. You've done some fading and sliding, but nothing more—until now. jQuery has a fully-featured animation library, but it comes with its quirks: sometimes things don't entirely happen as you might expect. This chapter will cover those "gotchas" and a lot more, including:

- jQuery's `animate()` method, which allows you to animate a large number of properties.

- More jQuery convenience methods, such as `fadeOut()`, `slideIn()`, and so on.

- jQuery's animation queue, which dictates how and when animations are run. They are not always run as you might expect.

- Common mistakes beginners make with animation—and how to avoid these mistakes.

- Enhancing the animation on your accordion so that it is less buggy.

- The infamous jQuery project: an image slider.

This is going to be a fairly heavy chapter. The image slider will combine everything you've learned so far. Let's get started!

The animate( ) Method

The `animate()` method can be used to animate a number of properties on an element over a period of time.

Basic Usage

The jQuery API has a succinct explanation of which properties can be animated:

> *All animated properties should be animated to a single numeric value, except as noted; most properties that are non-numeric cannot be animated using basic jQuery functionality (for example, width, height, or left can be animated but background-color cannot be, unless the jQuery.Color plugin is used). Property values are treated as a number of pixels unless otherwise specified. The units em and % can be specified where applicable. (http://api.jquery.com/animate/)*

© Jack Franklin, Russ Ferguson 2017
J. Franklin, R. Ferguson, *Beginning jQuery*, https://doi.org/10.1007/978-1-4842-3027-5_7

Plug-ins are available to animate complex properties such as color, but you'll usually animate something that has a distinct value, such as a width or height. The basic use of animate() has a very similar syntax to the css() method:

```
animate({
  property: value,
  property2: value2
}, 500);
```

More often than not, that's the form you'll use with the method. It takes an object of key-value pairs that relate properties to values.

The second argument is the duration in time. As with the convenience methods, this can be fast, normal, or slow—which are shortcuts for 200, 400, and 600 milliseconds, respectively. Otherwise, specify a value in milliseconds. If you don't specify a duration, 400 seconds (or "normal") is used as the default.

You are also able to pass in another argument, a callback function, which you have already used a few times in this book. When working with animations, a callback function is a function that is executed once the animation ends.

You might be wondering why you can't simply call animate() and then run some code like this:

```
$("div").animate({ "height": 50 }, 500);
$("p").text("animation finished");
```

The reasoning behind this comes down to how jQuery deals with animation. It doesn't just run the animation and then move to the next line. It gets the animation started, and then moves to the next line, while the animation is in progress—hence the need for using callbacks. You will examine this in more detail shortly.

Adding a callback function is really simple:

```
animate({
  property: value,
  property2: value2
}, 500, function() {
  console.log("finished");
});
```

Within the callback function, the value of this will refer to the DOM element that has just been animated. If you wanted to use jQuery methods on that object, you'd simply pass it through to jQuery, as follows: $(this).

Easing

Animations in jQuery support *easing functions*, which specify the speed that the animation should run at different points within an animation. For example, you might choose to have the animation move quickly for all but the last few moments, where you might slow it down so that it eases into its final position. By default, jQuery supports just two easing methods: linear and swing. Swing is the default, so if you don't name a particular easing method, swing will be used.

Figure 7-1 shows the difference between swing and linear. The higher line is *swing* and the lower is *linear*. The x axis is time and the y axis is distance.

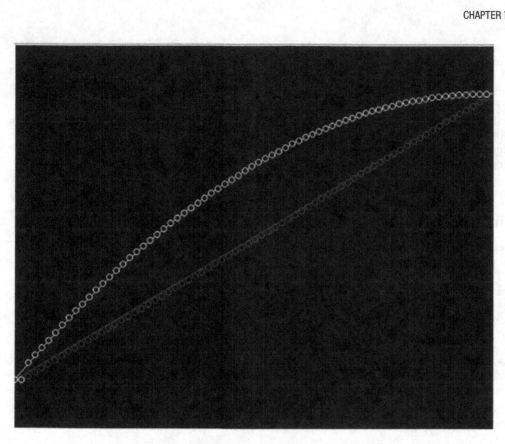

Figure 7-1. *A graph showing how the animation progresses by comparing "swing" and "linear"*

This graph was taken from James Padolsey's jQuery Easing; Illustrated (https://j11y.io/demos/jquery/easing/), which is a great web site for viewing all the different easing effects. You can see that there is a subtle difference between the two: linear goes at a constant rate, while swing starts slowly and then speeds up before easing down again.

Further easing effects are built into the jQuery UI (user interface) project (http://jqueryui.com). The jQuery UI project is a set of jQuery plug-ins for common UI components, but it also contains extra jQuery add-ons, including a set of easing effects. Later, you will use some of the extra easing functions, but for now, look at how you can animate with the linear function, rather than the default swing:

```
$("div").animate({
  "height": 500
}, 500, "linear");
```

The easing method to use simply goes as the third argument into the animate() function. This is demonstrated by the jQuery documentation for animate():

```
animate( properties [, duration] [, easing] [, complete] )
```

This shows that the `animate()` method can take up to four arguments. The arguments in square brackets are optional. jQuery is clever enough to figure out the arguments that you pass in and those that you don't. If you want to pass in a callback function, as well as the easing function to use, simply add it as the last argument:

```
$("div").animate({
  "height": 500
}, 500, "linear", function() {
  console.log("finished!");
});
```

Passing in Two Objects

Things can get a little confusing when passing in so many arguments, so you can pass in a second object for the other arguments:

```
$("div").animate({
  "height": 500
}, {
  "duration": 500,
  "easing": "linear",
  "complete":  function() { console.log("finished!"); }
});
```

Within the second object, there's no need to define the arguments in any order. Passing them in by name makes it a bit easier to see what's going on. Some prefer this, others don't. It tends to be a personal preference.

Animation Shortcuts

The majority of the time, you'll be animating a value—height, width, opacity, or otherwise. I most commonly animate to a specific height, perhaps to show extra information when a user hovers over a link or when making content slide in for visual effect:

```
$("div").animate({ "height": 300 }, 500);
```

Often, however, you'll commonly be animating to a height relative to the element's original height. You might need to expand an element to show more text, or if the element contains a text area to allow input, the user might need to expand the text box to accommodate the message. jQuery lets you animate like this:

```
$("div").animate({ "height": "+=200px" }, 500);
```

This animates the div to 200 pixels more than it started with. You can also use "-=" to animate it to 200 less than it started with.

Of course, you're not limited to pixel animation. jQuery presumes that you're animating by pixels, but you can animate by ems, percentage, or any other valid unit. Just specify it, like so:

```
$("div").animate({ "height" : "+=10%" }, 500);
```

Now that you're more comfortable with animation methods, take a look at some of the more popular convenience methods and what they animate.

More Convenience Methods

You've met the most common convenience methods, but before you dive further into animation, it's a good idea to review them—so that you know what they actually do and that you're comfortable using them. This shouldn't take long because most convenience methods follow the same pattern and they can be called in two ways:

```
methodName(duration, callback);

methodName(duration, easing, callback);
```

All three arguments are optional. All the upcoming methods follow this pattern, unless mentioned otherwise.

■ **Note**   Convenience methods also set the element's `display` property. For example, when `fadeOut()` runs, it animates the opacity down to 0 and then sets the display property to `"none"`. However `animate()` does not do this. It will only animate what you ask it to, and nothing more.

Fading

The fade methods are used to fade elements by animating their `opacity` property. They are as follows:

- `fadeIn();`
- `fadeOut();`
- `fadeToggle();`
- `fadeTo();`

The only method that varies is `fadeTo()`. It takes an extra required parameter, which is the opacity value to fade an element. This is given as a number between 0 (transparent) and 1 (fully opaque). Because the opacity is the second argument, this means that the duration must be also provided:

```
$("div").fadeTo(500, 0.5);
```

This is a bit unintuitive and may trip you up a couple of times, but you'll soon get used to it.

Sliding

The slide methods mirror the fade methods, with the one omission being no matching "slideTo" method. This is because it's incredibly rare that you would want to animate an element to a height that's not either 0 or its initial height. Remember, if none of the convenience methods do exactly what you need, simply use `animate()`. These methods are only handy wrappers around the `animate()` method in order to provide shortcuts to common functionality.

- `slideUp();`
- `slideDown();`
- `slideToggle();`

■ **Note**   If you ever find yourself checking whether an element is visible or not before sliding/fading it in, use the toggle methods to save yourself some work.

Sliding and Fading

jQuery also has three lesser-used methods to show and hide elements:

- show()
- hide()
- toggle()

Called without any arguments, they show or hide an element instantly. However, if you pass in any arguments, they turn into animations that animate the width, height, and opacity simultaneously. The methods take the same arguments as the slide and fade methods: either a duration and a callback, or a duration, an easing, and a callback.

The Animation Queue

When you run multiple animations on a single element, they are not all run at the same time but are added to jQuery's animation queue. You can see this in action through an example.

Create a new index.html file and fill it with the following:

```html
<!DOCTYPE html>
<html>
  <head>
    <title>Chapter 07, Exercise 01</title>
    <script src="jquery.js"></script>
    <script src="app.js"></script>
    <link rel="stylesheet" type="text/css" href="style.css" />
  </head>
  <body>
    <div id="box">
      box!
    </div>
  </body>
</html>
```

Style the div in order to make it easier to see what's going on:

```css
#box {
  width: 500px;
  height: 500px;
  background: blue;
}
```

Then add the following code to `app.js`:

```
$(function() {
  $("div")
    .animate({ "height" : 300 })
    .fadeOut()
    .show(500)
    .animate({ "width" : 100 })
    .css("background", "red");
});
```

Open `index.html` in a browser. You will see the background of the `div` change to red *before* the animations finish. This is because jQuery queues animations to run one after the other.

The browser only has one thread, which means it can only run one bit of code at a time. Applications with multiple threads are able to run multiple chunks of code at different times, meaning they can do more than one thing at once. Being multithreaded allows tasks to be executed asynchronously, rather than synchronously. In the browser, this isn't possible. If a bit of code runs for a long time, the user isn't able to use the browser because that bit of code runs and *blocks* the thread.

To get around this, jQuery does some workarounds with its animations to ensure that they are nonblocking so that the user is able to interact with the page while the animations run. When you call `animate()`—or any method that calls `animate()`—that animation is added to a queue. This queue is a *first in/first out* (FIFO) queue, which means animations are added to the queue and then run in the order they were added. Once an animation ends, it will trigger the next animation in the queue, if it exists.

This is why the `div`'s background changes to red very quickly. The first animation starts to run, and then all the others are added to the queue, meaning that the call to the `css()` method actually happens almost as soon as the first animation starts.

jQuery performs animation through a series of `setTimeout()` calls. `setTimeout()` is a JavaScript method that runs code after a defined time interval. When you run code to animate a `div`'s opacity from 1 to 0, it actually makes a large number of very small changes to the opacity over time to emulate an animation. There's no actual fading occurring. It's just very quickly changing the opacity by a small amount to give the illusion of animation.

A Common Problem

A common issue with this queue is the build-up of animations. Next, you'll build some code that will animate a `div` every time a header is clicked so that you can see this in action.

Create an `index.html` file with the following:

```
<!DOCTYPE html>
<html>
  <head>
    <title>Chapter 07, Exercise 02</title>
    <script src="jquery.js"></script>
    <script src="app.js"></script>
    <link rel="stylesheet" type="text/css" href="style.css" />
  </head>
  <body>
    <h5>Animate</h5>
    <div id="box">
      box!
    </div>
  </body>
</html>
```

Add some styling in `style.css`:

```css
#box {
  width: 500px;
  height: 500px;
  background: blue;
}
```

And JavaScript in `app.js`:

```javascript
$(function() {
  $("h5").on("click", function() {
    $("div").fadeToggle(500);
  });
});
```

If you run this and click the heading, you will see the `div` fade out. Another click will fade it back in. Now try clicking the heading multiple times—really quickly. You'll see the queue in action. The animations will build up, and when you stop clicking, the animations still run, creating the lag effect. If you want to avoid this effect, you need a way of clearing the queue every time a new animation is run. Thankfully, the jQuery developers thought of this, too, and provided the `stop()` method (http://api.jquery.com/stop/).

The `stop()` method lets you clear all queued animations. To avoid a buildup, you can clear the current queue before adding a new animation to it, meaning you'll never be in a situation where you have the lag effect.

First, try changing your `app.js` file to the following:

```javascript
$(function() {
  $("h5").on("click", function() {
    $("div").stop().fadeToggle(500);
  });
});
```

Try clicking the header multiple times. This doesn't quite do what you want. As the jQuery API explains: "When `.stop()` is called on an element, the currently-running animation (if any) is immediately stopped."

If you click it lots of times, the `div` stops being animated at a random point in the animation. When `stop()` is called with no arguments, the current animation immediately stops and the next one in the queue starts. Chances are that you'll want to finish the current animation before clearing the queue. As of jQuery 1.7, the `stop()` method takes three optional arguments: `queue`, `clearQueue`, and `jumpToEnd`, the last two of which are Boolean values defaulting to `false`.

The first argument is a string that represents the name of the queue that holds the animations you want to stop. If you pass in `true` as the second argument, jQuery will clear the entire animation queue, getting rid of the backlog.

If you pass in `true` for the third argument, jQuery will immediately skip to the end of the animation. So if the `div` is midway through fading in when `stop()` is called with `true` as the second argument, the `div` will immediately become fully faded in.

You need a combination of both of these:

```javascript
$(function() {
  $("h5").on("click", function() {
    $("div").stop(true, true).fadeToggle(500);
  });
});
```

Run the page in a browser and click frequently. As you click, you clear the queue and end the current animation, leading to no buildup and thus preventing the lag. In any complex sliding functionality, you'll most likely use `stop(true, true)`.

This is also why callbacks are so important in animations—they are the only way to be certain that the code within them will only run when an animation is complete. When you call `stop()` with no arguments, *the callback function is not called*. A callback function is only called when an animation has finished. If you call stop with the second argument as true—making the animation complete immediately when `stop()` is called, *the callback is called* because the animation finished, even if it had to do it quicker than expected.

A similar method to `stop()` is `finish()`. Added in jQuery 1.9, it finishes all currently running animations and removes everything in the queue. The one big difference between the methods is that whereas `stop()` sets the values of the current animation and removes everything that is in queue, finish() sets all the properties of the queued animations to the end values.

Fixing Your Accordion

The preceding problem is one your accordion suffers from, too. Let's recap where you were with your accordion at the end of Chapter 6. Here's the index.html:

```
<!DOCTYPE html>
<html>
  <head>
    <title>Chapter 06, Accordion</title>
    <script src="jquery.js"></script>
    <script src="app.js"></script>
    <link rel="stylesheet" type="text/css" href="style.css" />
  </head>
  <body>
    <div id="accordion">
      <h2>Heading</h2>
      <p>Lorem ipsum dolor sit amet, consectetur adipisicing elit, sed do eiusmod tempor
      incididunt ut labore et dolore magna aliqua. Ut enim ad minim veniam, quis nostrud
      exercitation ullamco laboris nisi ut aliquip ex ea commodo consequat. Duis aute irure
      dolor in reprehenderit in voluptate velit esse cillum dolore eu fugiat nulla pariatur.
      Excepteur sint occaecat cupidatat non proident, sunt in culpa qui officia deserunt
      mollit anim id est laborum.</p>
      <h2>Heading 2</h2>
      <p>Lorem ipsum dolor sit amet, consectetur adipisicing elit, sed do eiusmod tempor
      incididunt ut labore et dolore magna aliqua. Ut enim ad minim veniam, quis nostrud
      exercitation ullamco laboris nisi ut aliquip ex ea commodo consequat. Duis aute irure
      dolor in reprehenderit in voluptate velit esse cillum dolore eu fugiat nulla pariatur.
      Excepteur sint occaecat cupidatat non proident, sunt in culpa qui officia deserunt
      mollit anim id est laborum.</p>
      <h2>Heading 3</h2>
      <p>Lorem ipsum dolor sit amet, consectetur adipisicing elit, sed do eiusmod tempor
      incididunt ut labore et dolore magna aliqua. Ut enim ad minim veniam, quis nostrud
      exercitation ullamco laboris nisi ut aliquip ex ea commodo consequat. Duis aute irure
      dolor in reprehenderit in voluptate velit esse cillum dolore eu fugiat nulla pariatur.
      Excepteur sint occaecat cupidatat non proident, sunt in culpa qui officia deserunt
      mollit anim id est laborum.</p>
    </div>
  </body>
</html>
```

And some quick styling in `style.css`:

```css
#accordion {
  width: 500px;
  border: 1px solid black;
}

#accordion h2 {
  padding: 5px;
  margin: 0;
  background: #ddd;
}

#accordion p {
  padding: 0 5px;
}
```

And here's the JavaScript guilty of the lag problem:

```javascript
$(function() {
  var accordion = $("#accordion");
  var headings = $("h2");
  var paragraphs = $("p");
  paragraphs.not(":first").hide();
  accordion.on("click", "h2", function() {
    var t = $(this);
    var tPara = t.next();
    if(!tPara.is(":visible")) {
      tPara.trigger("showParagraph");
    }
  });

  accordion.on("showParagraph", "p", function() {
    paragraphs.slideUp("normal");
    $(this).slideDown("normal");
  });
});
```

Due to the gaps between the headers, it's actually very difficult to click enough times to cause any huge lag because you don't animate a paragraph that's already visible. This means that it's tough to click different headings to cause the lag, because clicking the same heading doesn't do anything once that section is visible. Fix any possibility of the "lag" effect by changing the function bound to the showParagraph event you trigger:

```javascript
accordion.on("showParagraph", "p", function() {
  paragraphs.stop(true, true).slideUp("normal");
  $(this).stop(true, true).slideDown("normal");
});
```

Next, try out a couple of the different easing options. As explained earlier, most of these exist in jQuery UI, so you need to include it to gain access to them. However, it would be a huge waste of space to include the entire jQuery UI library just for its easing functions. Thankfully, the web site lets you put together a custom build with only the bits that you need (http://jqueryui.com/download/), as shown in Figure 7-2.

Effects		
☑ Toggle All	☑ Effects Core	Extends the internal jQuery effects. Includes morphing and easing. Required by all other effects.
A rich effect API and ready to use effects.	☑ Blind Effect	Blinds the element.
	☑ Bounce Effect	Bounces an element horizontally or vertically n times.
	☑ Clip Effect	Clips the element on and off like an old TV.
	☑ Drop Effect	Moves an element in one direction and hides it at the same time.
	☑ Explode Effect	Explodes an element in all directions into n pieces. Implodes an element to its original wholeness.
	☑ Fade Effect	Fades the element.
	☑ Fold Effect	Folds an element first horizontally and then vertically.
	☑ Highlight Effect	Highlights the background of an element in a defined color for a custom duration.
	☑ Puff Effect	Creates a puff effect by scaling the element up and hiding it at the same time.
	☑ Pulsate Effect	Pulsates an element n times by changing the opacity to zero and back.
	☑ Scale Effect	Grows or shrinks an element and its content.
	☑ Shake Effect	Shakes an element horizontally or vertically n times.
	☑ Size Effect	Resize an element to a specified width and height.
	☑ Slide Effect	Slides an element in and out of the viewport.
	☑ Transfer Effect	Displays a transfer effect from one element to another.

Figure 7-2. The jQuery UI custom builds page

The only thing you need to tick is Effects Core. Don't worry about ticking any other boxes or filling out the Theme at the bottom of the page. Once you click the Download button, you get a zip file. Once you extract the zip file, you'll see a folder structure like that shown in Figure 7-3.

```
▼  jquery-ui-1.12.1.custom
      AUTHORS.txt
      index.html
      jquery-ui.css
      jquery-ui.js
      jquery-ui.min.css
      jquery-ui.min.js
      jquery-ui.structure.css
      jquery-ui.structure.min.css
      LICENSE.txt
      package.json
   ►  external
   jquery-ui-1.12.1.custom.zip
```

Figure 7-3. The resulting download from the jQuery UI custom build page

The file you need (as of this writing) is called `jquery-ui-1.12.1.custom.min.zip`. Unzip the file and use the "jquery-ui-min.js". This is the custom build, but minified for you. Copy it into your project folder and rename it to something shorter, such as simply `jqueryui.js`.

Go into `index.html` and edit the top, adding a link to include `jquery-ui-min.js` file. Make sure you do so after the jQuery source because jQuery UI, unsurprisingly, depends on jQuery:

```
<script src="jquery.js"></script>
<script src="jqueryui.js"></script>
<script src="app.js"></script>
<link rel="stylesheet" type="text/css" href="style.css" />
```

To view all the easing options now available to you, check out the jQuery UI documentation page (https://api.jqueryui.com/easings/). Give "easeInBack" a go:

```
accordion.on("showParagraph", "p", function() {
  paragraphs.stop(true, true).slideUp("normal", "easeInBack");
  $(this).stop(true, true).slideDown("normal", "easeInBack");
});
```

Feel free to try out a few and find your favorite. In the end, we settled on "easeInCirc":

```
accordion.on("showParagraph", "p", function() {
  paragraphs.stop(true, true).slideUp(1000, "easeInCirc");
  $(this).stop(true, true).slideDown(1000, "easeInCirc");
});
```

This code has a lot of duplication. The two lines look very similar, and if you want to change the duration or easing, you have to change it on two lines. That's never a good sign. It's times like this that you should look to abstract out into a utility function:

```
var animateAccordion = function(elem, duration, easing) {
  paragraphs.stop(true, true).slideUp(duration, easing);
  $(elem).stop(true, true).slideDown(duration, easing);
}
```

The function takes three arguments: `elem`, which refers to the element you want to slide down, and `duration` and `easing`. It then does the same animations as before, sliding all the paragraphs up and the active element down. This really tidies the event handler:

```
accordion.on("showParagraph", "p", function() {
  animateAccordion(this, 600, "easeInCirc");
});
```

It might not look like much of a change, but making things as easy as possible is really important in our opinion. We tend to refer to these small functions as "utility functions." They save a lot of time and typing in the long run—and you'll almost certainly find uses for them in future projects.

The Image Slider

It's time to take a first pass at building an image slider.

Before you dive into the code, you need to think about how you need it to work. You'll also have to do a little CSS work before you can get into the JavaScript. The list of images will be represented as an unordered list. You then style the images so that they are laid out horizontally. You make the list as wide as it needs to be to accommodate them all. Next, this unordered list sits within a div that is only as wide as one image and has its overflow property set to hidden. This way, only the current image is shown. You then manipulate the margin of the unordered list to animate the images.

It's all pretty straightforward. It just sounds worse than it is!

Start with the initial setup. Create a new directory and drop the jQuery source file in. You'll also want index.html, style.css, and app.js files.

Add the following to your index.html:

```html
<!DOCTYPE html>
<html>
  <head>
    <title>Chapter 07 Slider</title>
    <script src="jquery.js"></script>
    <script src="app.js"></script>
    <link rel="stylesheet" type="text/css" href="style.css" />
  </head>
  <body>
    <div id="slider">
      <ul>
        <li><img src=" https://unsplash.it/300/300/?random " alt="Random Image" /></li>
        <li><img src=" https://unsplash.it/300/300/?random " alt="Random Image" /></li>
        <li><img src=" https://unsplash.it/300/300/?random " alt="Random Image" /></li>
        <li><img src=" https://unsplash.it/300/300/?random " alt="Random Image" /></li>
        <li><img src=" https://unsplash.it/300/300/?random " alt="Random Image" /></li>
      </ul>
    </div>
  </body>
</html>
```

We're using the rather awesome Unsplash It web site (http://unsplash.it) to provide the placeholder images. They are represented within list items. You need to style these, so add the following to your style.css:

```css
#slider {
  width: 300px;
  height: 300px;
}
```

```
#slider ul {
  list-style: none;
  width: 1500px;
  height: 300px;
  margin: 0;
  padding: 0;
}
#slider li {
  float: left;
  width: 300px;
  height: 300px;
}
```

If you look at the page, you should see all of your images in a line going off the page, as shown in Figure 7-4.

Figure 7-4. *Random images, aligned in a row following the small CSS additions*

You can fix that by adding overflow: hidden; to the #slider div, as shown next. When you do that, you get just one random image, as expected (see Figure 7-5).

```
#slider {
  width: 300px;
  overflow: hidden;
  height: 400px;
}
```

Figure 7-5. *Once overflow: hidden; is added, only the first random image is visible.*

Finally, add buttons to let the user navigate forward and back through your slider. Add these just after the closing tag for the unordered list:

```
<span class="button back">Back</span>
<span class="button next">Next</span>
```

And then style them:

```
.button {
  font-family: Arial, sans-serif;
  font-size: 14px;
  display: block;
  padding: 6px;
  border: 1px solid #ccc;
  margin: 10px 0 0 0;
}

.back {
  float: left;
}
.next {
  float: right;
}
```

Also give the body a bit of padding, just to move the slider in slightly so that it's easier to see:

```
body {
  padding: 50px;
}
```

All that styling leaves you ready to JavaScript. Your image slider and buttons should look something like Figure 7-6.

Figure 7-6. *The fully styled image slider and buttons, ready to be implemented*

Whenever you're tackling a problem that's fairly complex, consider listing out all the functionality that you need, and then implement it, one bit at a time. Here's what you need to do:

- When the Back button is clicked, animate the unordered list to increase its margin by 300 pixels (the width of one image).

- When the Next button is clicked, animate the unordered list to decrease the margin by 300 pixels.

- Disable the Back button if at the first image.

- Disable the Next button if at the last image.

Once you've done all that, you will look at adding functionality that is more complex. The preceding is plenty to keep you going, however. So, let's get started!

First, store some variables that you'll no doubt have to refer to:

```
$(function() {
  var sliderWrapper = $("#slider");
  var sliderList = sliderWrapper.children("ul");
  var sliderItems = sliderList.children("li");
  var buttons = sliderWrapper.children(".button");
});
```

Next, make a function that will animate your slider. It will take two arguments: the direction in which to animate, which is either "+" or "-", and the duration the animation should take. Here's an example:

```
var animateSlider = function(direction, duration) {
  if(direction === "+") {
    sliderList.animate({
      "margin-left" : "+=300px"
    }, duration);
  } else {
    sliderList.animate({
      "margin-left" : "-=300px"
    }, duration);
  }
};
```

It's a pretty simple function that just animates the margin up or down by 300 pixels, depending on whether the direction argument is "+" or "-". There's certainly room for some refactoring here—there's a lot of duplicated code—but the focus now is to get a basic implementation working, and then revisit the code.

Now that you have this function, you need to run it when the buttons are clicked. That's also simple:

```
buttons.on("click", function() {
  if($(this).hasClass("back")) {
    animateSlider("+", 1000);
  } else {
    animateSlider("-", 1000);
  };
});
```

If you refresh the page, you have a working slider in place! You've only got your first two bullet points done, but congratulations—you have implemented a basic image slider! That wasn't so bad, really. Before you move to the next two bullet points, do some refactoring, particularly in the animateSlider() method:

```
var animateSlider = function(direction, duration) {
  if(direction == "+") {
    sliderList.animate({
      "margin-left" : "+=300px"
    }, duration);
  } else {
    sliderList.animate({
      "margin-left" : "-=300px"
    }, duration);
  }
};
```

The duplication here is horrible. You only want to have the call to animate appear once. It turns out there's an easy way to fix this:

```
var animateSlider = function(direction, duration) {
  sliderList.animate({
    "margin-left" : direction + "=300px"
  }, duration);
};
```

As you pass in the direction, you just append the "=300px" to the direction variable, which will give you either "+=300px" or "-=300px", which is exactly what you need. That's much better.

Now take look at the click event handler on the buttons:

```
buttons.on("click", function() {
 if($(this).hasClass("back")) {
    animateSlider("+", 1000);
  } else {
    animateSlider("-", 1000);
  };
});
```

Again, calling animateSlider() twice is messy. There's a nice solution here to trim the event handler down to just a one-liner:

```
buttons.on("click", function() {
  animateSlider(($(this).hasClass("back") ? "+" : "-"), 1000);
});
```

Here you've used a *ternary operator*. Take a moment to study it a bit more closely:

```
($(this).hasClass("back") ? "+" : "-")
```

This is simply a syntactical shortcut for

```
if($(this).hasClass("back")) { return "+" } else { return "-" }
```

The bit to the left of the question mark is evaluated to either true or false. If it's true, the item after the question mark is returned. If it's false, the bit after the colon is returned. So here, if the button has a class of "back", it will return "+"; but if it does not have that class, it will return "-". Be careful here. Although you're going back, you are actually animating the margin positively—even though it seems counterintuitive at first.

This leaves your entire slider looking much tidier. All that functionality in just 16 lines of code!

```
$(function() {
  var sliderWrapper = $("#slider");
  var sliderList = sliderWrapper.children("ul");
  var sliderItems = sliderList.children("li");
  var buttons = sliderWrapper.children(".button");

  var animateSlider = function(direction, duration) {
    sliderList.animate({
      "margin-left" : direction + "=300px"
    }, duration);
  };
```

```
buttons.on("click", function() {
    animateSlider(($(this).hasClass("back") ? "+" : "-"), 1000);
  });
});
```

The new problem is that you can click either button infinitely, and the margin will still be animated, leaving a blank space where the image should be.

If the margin of the unordered list is set to 0, it means you are at the first image, and hence the Back button should be disabled. If the margin is set to –1200 pixels, you are at the last image. This value is simply the width of an image, multiplied by the number of images you have. First, write a helper function to tell you if the slider is at the beginning:

```
var isAtStart = function() {
  return parseInt(sliderList.css("margin-left"), 10) === 0;
};
```

This uses a new JavaScript method called parseInt(), which you have not yet seen. It takes a string and turns it into an integer. For the string "300px", it will return the integer 300. The second parameter that it takes is the radix of the string. This is optional, but it's highly recommended that you use it to guarantee expected results. More often than not, you'll use base 10. If the margin is 0, you're at the start; if it's not 0, you're not at the start, so you can simply return parseInt(sliderList.css("margin-left"), 10) == 0 as the result. It gets evaluated to either true or false.

Now rework the event handler. Here's an example of how to do it:

```
buttons.on("click", function() {
  var $this = $(this);
  var isBackBtn = $this.hasClass("back");
  if(isBackBtn && isAtStart()) {
    return;
  }
  animateSlider(( isBackBtn ? "+" : "-"), 1000);
});
```

This stores the result of $this.hasClass("back") because it's probable that you'll reference it at least twice. Then, if isBackBtn is true and isAtStart() is also true, you simply return, which returns and stops any further execution of the event handler. This ensures that the Back button doesn't work when you get to the beginning.

Next, do the same for when the user clicks the Back button when at the end of the slider:

```
var isAtEnd = function() {
  var imageWidth = sliderItems.first().width();
  var imageCount = sliderItems.length;
  var maxMargin = -1 * (imageWidth * (imageCount-1));
  return parseInt(sliderList.css("margin-left"), 10) === maxMargin;
}
```

You have to do a bit more work here. First, calculate the width of an image by getting the width of an individual list item. The maximum margin is the width of an item multiplied by the number of images, minus one. This is because at a margin of 0, the first image is displayed; so at –300 pixels, it's showing the second image, not the first. You return if the slider margin is indeed the maximum margin. Your event handler becomes

```
buttons.on("click", function() {
  var $this = $(this);
  var isBackBtn = $this.hasClass("back");
  if(isBackBtn && isAtStart()) {
    return;
  }
  if(!isBackBtn && isAtEnd()) {
    return;
  }
  animateSlider(( isBackBtn ? "+" : "-"), 1000);
});
```

But you can merge those conditionals together using the or (||) operator:

```
buttons.on("click", function() {
  var $this = $(this);
  var isBackBtn = $this.hasClass("back");
  if( (isBackBtn && isAtStart()) || (!isBackBtn && isAtEnd()) ) { return; }
  animateSlider(( isBackBtn ? "+" : "-"), 1000);
});
```

Note that this also brings up the return statement and the braces onto the same line, simply because having just the word "return" on its own line seems like a foolish waste of space. Your four bullet points are done—all in 31 lines of JavaScript:

```
$(function() {
  var sliderWrapper = $("#slider");
  var sliderList = sliderWrapper.children("ul");
  var sliderItems = sliderList.children("li");
  var buttons = sliderWrapper.children(".button");

  var animateSlider = function(direction, duration) {
    sliderList.animate({
      "margin-left" : direction + "=300px"
    }, duration);
  };

  var isAtStart = function() {
    return parseInt(sliderList.css("margin-left"), 10) === 0;
  };

  var isAtEnd = function() {
    var imageWidth = sliderItems.first().width();
    var imageCount = sliderItems.length;
    var maxMargin = -1 * (imageWidth * (imageCount-1));
    return parseInt(sliderList.css("margin-left"), 10) === maxMargin;
  }

  buttons.on("click", function() {
    var $this = $(this);
    var isBackBtn = $this.hasClass("back");
```

```
    if( (isBackBtn && isAtStart()) || (!isBackBtn && isAtEnd()) ) { return; }
    animateSlider(( isBackBtn ? "+" : "-"), 1000);
  });

});
```

And there you have the basic JavaScript slider.

There's one final thing to cover before ending this chapter: the animation lag problem. You also want to be able to pass in a callback to the animateSlider() function, because when you improve this slider later (you'll turn it into a plug-in), it might come in handy:

```
var animateSlider = function(direction, duration, callback) {
  sliderList.stop(true, true).animate({
    "margin-left" : direction + "=300px"
  }, duration, callback);
};
```

All you need to do is call stop(true, true), which causes it to empty the animation queue and to immediately get to the end of the currently running animation before starting the next. Using a callback is easy: you just make your animateSlider() method take the argument and pass it through to the animate() method. If you don't need to use a callback, you don't have to pass one in. jQuery will see that the callback is undefined and will not try to execute it.

If you click the Next button a couple of times in succession, you'll see it's possible for you to click enough that it scrolls past the end. Why is this? It is because the isAtEnd() method only returns true if the margin is exactly –1200. But if you click the Next button during an animation, the margin is somewhere between –900 and –1200. So you actually want to check that the margin is less than (negative values, remember) –900, which is the imageWidth * (imageCount - 2):

```
var isAtEnd = function() {
  var imageWidth = sliderItems.first().width();
  var imageCount = sliderItems.length;
  var maxMargin = -1 * (imageWidth * (imageCount-2));
  return parseInt(sliderList.css("margin-left"), 10) < maxMargin;
}
```

That fixes that issue, but the Back button has similar problems. Again, you just need to check that the margin is greater than –300 pixels, rather than it being exactly zero.

```
var isAtStart = function() {
  return parseInt(sliderList.css("margin-left"), 10) > -300;
};
```

Now you have a slider that is far more robust.

Summary

There is still a lot of work to be done on your slider. You will see that when you turn it into a jQuery plug-in later in the book. As part of your process to turn it into a plug-in, you will refactor and rework it. You will also look at making it scroll infinitely and seamlessly.

Animation is a mammoth part of jQuery. This has been a big chapter: you've improved your accordion, written the most complex JavaScript thus far, and learned how jQuery's animations work behind the scenes.

CHAPTER 8

■ ■ ■

Ajax with jQuery

Ajax, which stands for *Asynchronous JavaScript and XML*, lets us fetch and send data to and from a server asynchronously, in the background, without interfering with the user's experience.

In Chapter 7, you saw examples of asynchronous behavior. While animations were running, you were able to execute other code, such as changing the element's background color, and the user (in this case, you) was perfectly able to use the page while the animations were taking place. Nothing seemed different, other than the animation. Fetching data with Ajax is much like that. As a user, you're unaware of what's happening until the data has been fetched and then shown on the page.

In this chapter, you'll thoroughly explore Ajax. Although Ajax stands for "Asynchronous JavaScript and XML," the most common format for getting data back is now JSON, or JavaScript Object Notation; before you start fetching data, you'll become familiar with this format. Next, you'll look at some sample JSON and see how to work with it using JavaScript. Then, you'll be introduced to jQuery's ajax() method. Finally, you'll use a real-world third-party API to pull in data and display it on a page. To do this, you'll need to explore JSONP, a method of requesting data from third-party web sites.

Ajax has been somewhat of a buzzword in recent years, but what it actually means can be confusing. It's simply a way of asynchronously fetching data. That's it.

JSON

The "x" in Ajax may stand for XML, but the format nearly everyone prefers these days is JSON, which stands for *JavaScript Object Notation* (http://json.org).

JSON data looks very similar to a regular JavaScript object. Here's an example:

```
"name":"Jack Franklin",
"age":20,
"location":"London, UK",
"friends":[
  "Grant",
  "Jamie",
  "Dan",
  "Richard",
  "Alex"
]
}
```

© Jack Franklin, Russ Ferguson 2017
J. Franklin, R. Ferguson, *Beginning jQuery*, https://doi.org/10.1007/978-1-4842-3027-5_8

There are two important things to note here. The first is that, unlike JavaScript, keys in a JSON object have to have double quotes around them. For example, in JavaScript, all of the following are valid:

```
var jack = { "age": 20 };
var jack = { 'age': 20 };
var jack = { age: 20 };
```

However, only the first line would be valid in JSON.

Values in JSON can be of the following types:

- String

- Number

- Array

- Boolean true/false

- null

Items in arrays can be any of these types, too. Strings need to be double quoted, but the rest don't:

```
{
    "num":2,
    "decimal":2.5,
    "boolean":true,
    "array":[
        1,
        2,
        3,
        true,
        null
    ]
}
```

Much like JavaScript objects, key-value pairs need a comma after them, unless it's the last pair in the object.

All current browsers come with native JS methods for parsing JSON. There are two main methods:

- `JSON.stringify()`: Takes a JavaScript object and produces a JSON string from it.

- `JSON.parse()`: Takes a JSON string and parses it to a JavaScript object.

The Can I Use web site (`http://caniuse.com/json`) shows all current browsers now natively support JSON (see Figure 8-1).

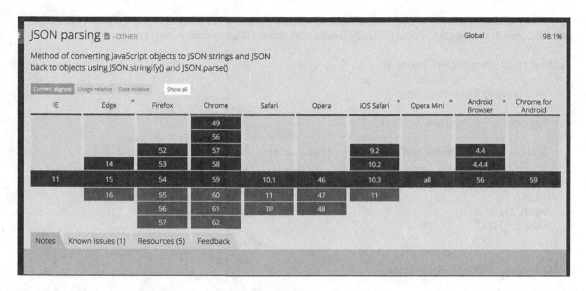

Figure 8-1. Table showing JSON support across multiple browsers

Parsing JSON in JavaScript

Start with a basic JSON string:

```
var json = '{ "person" : { "age" : 20, "name" : "Jack" } }';
```

Right now, all JavaScript sees here is a string. It doesn't know it's actually JSON. You can pass it through to JSON.parse() to convert it into a JavaScript object:

```
var parsed = JSON.parse(json);
console.log(parsed);
```

This gives you:

```
{ person:   { age: 20, name: 'Jack' } }
```

It is now a regular JavaScript object and you can access properties, just as you'd expect, using either notation:

```
console.log(parsed.person);
console.log(parsed.person["age"]);
```

This gives the following:

```
{ age: 20, name: 'Jack' }
20
```

If you get the JSON wrong, you'll see an error. Take the following invalid JSON, for example:

```
var invalid = '{ person: "Jack" }';
```

It's invalid because the key, `person`, should have quotes around it. Trying to run `JSON.parse(invalid)` gives this result in Google Chrome (other browsers may show a slightly different error message):

```
SyntaxError: Unexpected token p
```

This is easily fixed, as follows:

```
var invalid = '{ "person": "Jack" }';
```

You can do the opposite and turn an object into a string:

```
var json = {
  person: {
    age: 20,
    name: "Jack"
  }
}
console.log(JSON.stringify(json));
```

This gives you a string containing the following:

```
{"person":{"age":20,"name":"Jack"}}
```

When working with JSON responses from a jQuery Ajax call, you're not going to have to worry much about parsing the JSON. jQuery takes care of that for you.

Ajax with jQuery

jQuery comes with `jQuery.ajax()`, a complex and powerful method to handle Ajax requests (`http://api.jquery.com/jQuery.ajax/`). This method is different from others you've seen because you don't call it on a jQuery object containing elements, but on the jQuery object itself. Most methods are called on sets of elements; for example:

```
$("div").addClass("foo");
```

This calls the `addClass()` method on every element within the jQuery object `$("div")`, which is all the div elements on the page. With the `$.ajax()` method, however, you simply call

```
$.ajax(...)
```

Take a look at how you might make a request to a fictional URL to get some JSON. Later on, you will use an actual API, but for now, familiarize yourself with the method. With the `$.ajax()` method, you can pass in one argument, which is an object of options, or you can pass in two arguments. The first is the URL to pass in and the second is an object of options. We prefer the first method—passing in one object that contains a property for the URL, in which you would either do, for example:

```
$.ajax({
  "url": "/myurl",
  //more settings here
});
```

or

```
$.ajax("/myurl", { ... });
```

We prefer the first method because we think it's clearer to have every option within one object and to have each option on its own line. Hence, this is the style we'll use throughout the book. It's also the one we see most others use, which is another good reason for following suit. If you prefer the other syntax, however, feel free to use it.

The most important argument is the URL, which may be a local URL (on the same domain as your script) or an external URL (hosted on a different domain). There's a bit more work to be done if you want to use an external URL, so for now, presume it's a local URL that will return data in JSON format. You'll get to external URLs later.

The URL is relative to the page that the script is loaded into. This can vary depending on your site structure, so the best way to be confident which URL the script will hit is to make it an absolute URL—that is, put a "/" at the beginning so that the URL is relative to the domain root.

The list of properties that can be set has grown over the years. Refer to the documentation (https://api.jquery.com/jQuery.ajax/) for the full list.

Here we will outline a few important properties to illustrate how to use jQuery to make a request from the server.

After adding the URL you can also add type. This is the type of request to make. The default is GET, which is when you're making a request to *get* the data from the URL. The other is POST, which is when you want to send (or *post*) data to the server.

Next up is dataType, which denotes the type of data that is returned to you. jQuery is pretty clever here because it is able to fairly accurately guess, but we like to be explicit and set the dataType, nearly always to "json".

In order to see the success or failure of an Ajax call, you can chain the done() or fail() methods:

```
$.ajax({
"url" : 'https://jsonplaceholder.typicode.com/posts'
}).done(function(data){
    //if the call is successful
    console.log(data)
}).fail(function(jqXHR, textStatus, errorThrown){
    //if the call is not successful
}).always(function(){
    //runs all the time
});
```

■ **Note** As of jQuery 1.8, using error() and success() are deprecated, meaning they shouldn't be used; instead, use the following:

done(), which replaces success()

fail(), which replaces error()

always(), which runs regardless of whether the request was successful or not

---

It's important to again note that Ajax calls are asynchronous. When something is *asynchronous*, it runs in the background and it doesn't stop the rest of your code from executing. This is also known as *nonblocking*. Running something asynchronously makes it nonblocking because it doesn't stop the code below from executing. Something basic like a call to console.log is blocking because while it's running (albeit for a fraction of time), nothing else can run until it's finished.

When you make an Ajax request, the code immediately after the Ajax request code is run, regardless of whether or not your Ajax call has finished. When you looked at animations in Chapter 7, you had to use callback functions because the code below the animation would run immediately. Animations are also asynchronous, and just as you used a callback with animations, you can do so with Ajax. Thus, you can't just return your data within the function, because when the Ajax method is called, the data will take an arbitrary amount of time to get back to you, and it's happening while your other code is executing. Hence, you chain the function that you know will run only once you have the data. This is much like the callbacks you used in animating elements, which you knew would only run once the animation had finished.

Put all this together into an example. As always, get an index.html page, which for this example should just contain the following:

```html
<!DOCTYPE html>
<html>
  <head>
    <title>Chapter 08, Exercise 01</title>
    <script src="jquery.js"></script>
    <script src="app.js"></script>
  </head>
  <body>
  </body>
</html>
```

There's no need for any actual HTML elements or a style sheet. Next, create a file called sample.json. This will contain some JSON, which you will fetch via an Ajax request. Put the following inside it:

```json
  "people": [
    { "name": "Jack", "age" : 20 },
    { "name": "Grant", "age": 21 },
    { "name": "Lisa", "age": 21 }
  ]
}
```

That's a JSON object that contains an array of people with age and name properties. Implement the Ajax call in your app.js file. Notice how the following uses a url of /sample.json. This means the JSON file must sit within the project root directory. If it doesn't, or if you'd rather put it in a subdirectory, amend this.

```js
$(function() {
  $.ajax({
    "url": "/sample.json",
    "type": "get",
    "dataType": "json",
  }).done(function(results){
    console.log(results);
      });
});
```

Setting Up a Local Development Server

Because of the internals of Ajax, you won't be able to open the index.html file in a browser. You need to run the code on a local server for it to work properly. If you're on macOS you can run a simple HTTP server easily through Python, which is installed by default on macOS machines. Simply run the following through a terminal window within the directory of your project:

```
python -m SimpleHTTPServer
```

And then you can load http://localhost:8080 in a browser to view it. Another cross-platform way of setting up a local server is using Node.js. Node.js can be installed on all platforms. One way to get it is to go to https://nodejs.org. This will give you the runtime for your platform.

Once installed, Node.js includes a package manager. Node Package Manager (npm) allows you to download utilities built in JavaScript, which for purposes of this chapter will let you use Node.js as a local server.

To make your current folder the root of your web server, you will have to use Terminal on macOS or a command-line utility on Windows (Git Bash, for example). At the command line, navigate to the folder you want to serve and install the http-server module. Use the command npm install http-server –g. The –g flag means that this will be installed globally. You can set up any folder as a server once this is installed.

If you are not already at the folder you want to serve, make sure you navigate to it. Then launch the server by typing http-server. This will create a server that you can now open your browser and go to localhost:8080.

Once you've got that set up, view the site in your browser and open the developer tools. You should see something like Figure 8-2, which shows the Chrome developer tools, but all developer tools should show a similar output.

```
▼ Object {people: Array[3]}
  ▼ people: Array[3]
    ► 0: Object
    ▼ 1: Object
        age: 21
        name: "Grant"
      ► __proto__: Object
    ► 2: Object
      length: 3
    ► __proto__: Array[0]
  ► __proto__: Object
```

Figure 8-2. *The object parsed from the JSON that the Ajax call returned*

You can see that jQuery turns the JSON into an object—so you don't have to do the parsing stage. If you give the Ajax method the wrong URL, you'll see an error thrown, as shown in Figure 8-3.

```
⊗ ►GET http://localhost:8080/sa2mple.json 404 (Not Found)                    jquery.js:2
  fail                                                                         app.js:5
  ► (3) [Object, "error", "Not Found", callee: function, Symbol(Symbol.iterator): function]
  always                                                                       app.js:6
  ► (3) [Object, "error", "Not Found", callee: function, Symbol(Symbol.iterator): function]
>
```

Figure 8-3. *The error thrown if the Ajax URL is incorrect, shown in the Chrome developer tools console*

Now see what happens if you define the `fail()` method (see Figure 8-4):

```
$(function() {
  $.ajax({
    "url": "/sample2.json",
    "type": "get",
    "dataType": "json"
  }).fail(function(){
      console.log('fail', arguments);
  });
});
```

You can output the details as they are passed back through the `fail()` function, but we've never really found any huge use for it.

```
fail                                                                      app.js:5
▼ (3) [Object, "error", "Not Found", callee: function, Symbol(Symbol.iterator): function]
  ▶ 0: Object
    1: "error"
    2: "Not Found"
  ▶ callee: function ()
    length: 3
  ▶ Symbol(Symbol.iterator): function values()
  ▶ __proto__: Object
```

Figure 8-4. *The output from the fail() function, shown in the Chrome developer tools console*

Just like the `fadeIn()` and `fadeOut()` convenience-type methods that you saw with animations, there are some that exist for Ajax, too. You could use the `getJSON()` method (`http://api.jquery.com/jQuery.getJSON/`) to trim the preceding example to the following:

```
$(function() {
  $.getJSON("/sample.json", function(data) {
    console.log(data);
  });
});
```

This is equivalent to the following:

```
$.ajax({
  "url": "/sample.json",
  "dataType": "json"
}).done(function(){
});
```

So as you can see, it saves a little bit of work. You will notice that there's no error message defined. This is because `getJSON()` only supports defining a function if the Ajax request succeeded. You might decide this is acceptable, but it is best practice to deal with errors, so you might prefer, as we do, to stick to using `$.ajax()` directly, so you can define an error handler.

Thankfully, this all became easier post–jQuery 1.5 with *Deferreds* (*https://api.jquery.com/category/deferred-object/*), which are ways to manage callbacks in a much nicer way. Deferreds are very powerful, but you'll only need to scratch the surface for your Ajax work.

Let's take a moment to understand the jqXHR object. This is a wrapper around the browser's native XMLHttpRequest object—the way Ajax requests are done with just JavaScript, making life much easier for you. Every jQuery Ajax method—both the convenience ones like $.getJSON() and the main $.ajax() method—returns an instance of this object. What you can then do is add your callback methods onto this, meaning you don't have to define them within the call to the Ajax method. For example, rather than:

```
$.ajax({
  "url": "/someUrl",
  "success": function() {
    //before deferred objects
    //do something here
  }
});
```

you could do this:

```
var req = $.ajax({
  "url": "/someUrl"
});

req.done(function() {
  //do something
});
```

You save the returned value of $.ajax() (the jqXHR object) to a variable, and then you can declare callback functions on that, which is cleaner.

Take a look at the arguments that are passed into these functions, starting with done(response, status, jqXHR):

- response is the response from the server; typically, the JSON the server has responded to.

- status is a string denoting the status; with done(), it is nearly always "success".

- jqXHR returns the jqXHR object.

With fail(), the order is slightly different; it is the same order as the arguments in the error callback you used earlier:

```
.fail(jqXHR, status, errorThrown)
```

always() is passed the same arguments as .done() or fail(), depending on which one runs (they can never both run).

The real advantage of this is that you can set up multiple callbacks:

```
var req = $.ajax({
  "url": "/someUrl"
});
```

```
req.done(function() {
  //do something
});
req.done(function() {
  //do something else
});

req.always(function() {
  //always do this
});
```

This means that if you have more than one thing to do when you get data back, you can split it up into multiple functions to keep things more organized. The .always() callback is really useful for executing something regardless of the success or failure of the Ajax request. From this point on in the book, we'll be using this callback style, and we encourage you to do the same.

A Real API: TVmaze

TVmaze (http://www.tvmaze.com) is a web site for fans of all sorts of TV shows. This site also has a free and open API that returns results formatted as JSON objects. You can find the documentation at http://www.tvmaze.com/api.

If, for example, you wanted to get information on a TV show or a movie, you can use the URL provided with shows?q=showName, where the placeholder showName is be the name of the show you are searching for. This will return a JSON object with information such as ID, language, and summary. A search for the show "Gravity Falls" (http://api.tvmaze.com/search/shows?q=Gravity%20Falls) would return an object similar to what is shown in Figure 8-5.

```
▼ [{score: 38.48098,…}]
  ▼ 0: {score: 38.48098,…}
    score: 38.48098
    ▼ show: {id: 396, url: "http://www.tvmaze.com/shows/396/gravity-falls", name: "Gravity Falls",…}
      ► externals: {tvrage: 31839, thetvdb: 259972, imdb: "tt1865718"}
      ► genres: ["Adventure", "Mystery", "Supernatural"]
        id: 396
      ► image: {medium: "http://static.tvmaze.com/uploads/images/medium_portrait/2/6140.jpg",…}
        language: "English"
        name: "Gravity Falls"
      ► network: {id: 25, name: "Disney XD", country: {name: "United States", code: "US", timezone: "America/New_York
        officialSite: null
        premiered: "2012-06-15"
      ► rating: {average: 9.4}
        runtime: 30
      ► schedule: {time: "19:00", days: ["Monday"]}
        status: "Ended"
        summary: "<p>Twin brother and sister Dipper and Mabel Pines are in for an unexpected adventure when they sper
        type: "Animation"
        updated: 1476106577
        url: "http://www.tvmaze.com/shows/396/gravity-falls"
        webChannel: null
        weight: 87
      ► _links: {self: {href: "http://api.tvmaze.com/shows/396"},…}
```

Figure 8-5. *The results of a call to the TV Maze API, returned as a JSON object*

With this information, you can now make more specific requests. You can take the ID number and request all the episodes. The documentation uses `:id` as a placeholder. Making a call to `http://api. tvmaze.com/shows/:id/episodes` retrieves the episode list. The code would look like this:

```
$(function() {
  var req = $.ajax({
    url: " http://api.tvmaze.com/shows/396/episodes "
  });
  req.done(function(data) {
    console.log(data);
  });

});
```

Load the console to see what you get (see Figure 8-6).

```
▼ [{id: 39048, url: "http://www.tvmaze.com/episodes/39048/gravity-falls-1x01-tourist-trapped",…},…]
  ▼ 0: {id: 39048, url: "http://www.tvmaze.com/episodes/39048/gravity-falls-1x01-tourist-trapped",…}
      airdate: "2012-06-15"
      airstamp: "2012-06-15T21:55:00-04:00"
      airtime: "21:55"
      id: 39048
    ▶ image: {medium: "http://static.tvmaze.com/uploads/images/medium_landscape/15/37873.jpg",…}
      name: "Tourist Trapped"
      number: 1
      runtime: 30
      season: 1
      summary: "<p>When Dipper and Mabel Pines arrive to spend their summer break in the remote town of Gravity Fall
      url: "http://www.tvmaze.com/episodes/39048/gravity-falls-1x01-tourist-trapped"
    ▶ _links: {self: {href: "http://api.tvmaze.com/episodes/39048"}}
  ▶ 1: {id: 39049,…}
  ▶ 2: {id: 39050, url: "http://www.tvmaze.com/episodes/39050/gravity-falls-1x03-headhunters",…}
  ▶ 3: {id: 39051,…}
  ▶ 4: {id: 39052, url: "http://www.tvmaze.com/episodes/39052/gravity-falls-1x05-the-inconveniencing",…}
  ▶ 5: {id: 39053, url: "http://www.tvmaze.com/episodes/39053/gravity-falls-1x06-dipper-vs-manliness",…}
  ▶ 6: {id: 39054, url: "http://www.tvmaze.com/episodes/39054/gravity-falls-1x07-double-dipper",…}
  ▶ 7: {id: 39055, url: "http://www.tvmaze.com/episodes/39055/gravity-falls-1x08-irrational-treasure",…}
  ▶ 8: {id: 39056, url: "http://www.tvmaze.com/episodes/39056/gravity-falls-1x09-the-time-travelers-pig",…}
  ▶ 9: {id: 39057, url: "http://www.tvmaze.com/episodes/39057/gravity-falls-1x10-fight-fighters",…}
```

Figure 8-6. *A partial list of results from the network section of Chrome's developer tools*

There may be instances when a call to a remote server returns an error. It may look something like this: "XMLHttpRequest cannot load `http://api.mysite.com`. Origin `http://localhost:8000` is not allowed by Access-Control-Allow-Origin."

Be aware that not all browsers will explain why the Ajax request failed, but will only inform you that it did. If you're ever in doubt as to why a request failed, it's a good idea to load it up in a browser that you know will show you the errors more explicitly, such as Chrome's console.

This comes down to security. By default, the browser won't allow one domain to make an Ajax call to a URL on another domain to pull in data, because this could be potentially dangerous. The Mozilla Developer Network (https://developer.mozilla.org/en-US/docs/Web/HTTP/Access_control_CORS) explains it nicely:

> *A resource makes a **cross-origin HTTP request** when it requests a resource from a different domain, protocol, or port to its own. For example, an HTML page served from http://domain-a.com makes an <img> src request for http://domain-b.com/image.jpg. Many pages on the web today load resources like CSS stylesheets, images, and scripts from separate domains.*
>
> *For security reasons, browsers restrict cross-origin HTTP requests initiated from within scripts. For example, XMLHttpRequest and Fetch follow the same-origin policy. So, a web application using XMLHttpRequest or Fetch could only make HTTP requests to its own domain. To improve web applications, developers asked browser vendors to allow cross-domain requests.*

Of course, this is not practical when it comes to using third-party APIs, and hence, many workarounds exist. One workaround is Cross-Origin Resource Sharing (CORS), which allows the server to include a header in its response, stating that a cross-origin request is valid.

Another solution, the one commonly used today, is to use JSONP, which stands for *JSON Padded*. A blog post from Johnny Wey (https://johnnywey.wordpress.com/2012/05/20/jsonp-how-does-it-work/) explains it in detail, but this bit from the blog particularly gets to the essence of how it works:

> *The idea of JSONP is actually pretty simple: toss a script tag into the DOM with a reference to a resource that returns JSON data. Have the server return said JSON with "padding" (the "P" part of JSONP) that executes a function wrapping the incoming data.*

At this point, you may have realized something: you can't make requests to servers to get at JSON, but you're able to include external style sheets or scripts. For example, Chapter 1 showed you how to include the jQuery source from the Google CDN in a regular script tag:

```
<script src="http://ajax.googleapis.com/ajax/libs/jquery/3.2.1/jquery.min.js"></script>
```

What if you could put the URL of the data you want into a script tag and get the server's response as a JavaScript script, thus allowing you to get at the data? This is how JSONP works. Providing that the server supports it (and most popular APIs will), you can use it. It works by wrapping the response from the server in a function. For example, the server might respond with

```
someFunction(data);
```

data is the JSON data. That is then included as regular JavaScript in your page, and then you can define someFunction to process the data. That is how JSONP works. Thankfully, jQuery does all this for you to make it easier; so you don't need to worry about such specifics when working with jQuery, but it's good to know how things work.

So, how easy is it to get working in jQuery? Incredibly. Here is an example:

```
$(function() {
  var req = $.ajax({
    url: "http://api.remote-site.com/show/626625"
  });
  req.done(function(data) {
    console.log(data);
  });

});
```

Add the dataType property to the ajax call:

```
$(function() {
  var req = $.ajax({
    url: "http://api.remote-site.com/show/626625",
    dataType: "jsonp"
  });
  req.done(function(data) {
    console.log(data);
  });

});
```

Before continuing, there is one major caveat to JSONP that's worth mentioning, and that is that *error callbacks will not run if something goes wrong*. It is an unfortunate trade-off that you have to work around.

Summary

What a chapter!

- You were introduced to the concept of an Ajax request and showed how it works.

- You learned what the term "asynchronous" means.

- You became acquainted with JavaScript Object Notation (JSON).

- You examined problems with JSON and cross-origin requests, and how to overcome them using JSONP.

- You saw how to make Ajax calls with jQuery and the methods it provides.

- You made a request to an external API and got data back.

In the next chapter, we begin writing our first jQuery plugin.

CHAPTER 9

■ ■ ■

Writing a jQuery Plug-in

jQuery plug-ins are something that beginners tend to shy away from or are afraid to use. Plug-ins seem to be built up in people's minds as incredibly complex things to use, but once you learn how they work, you'll find them actually very straightforward, and you'll find yourself making multiple plug-ins while working. Plug-ins are not as complicated as you might think, as this chapter will demonstrate.

After exploring the benefits of the plug-in and when to turn code into one, you will learn about different types of plug-ins, build a few small plug-ins to see how they work, and discover how to make them more configurable to a potential developer. In the next chapter, you'll take code that you've previously written, including the accordion you started in Chapter 5 and the Ajax code from Chapter 8, and turn them into fully functioning plug-ins. You will then write a fully-featured, complex, image slider plug-in. But for now, we'll keep it simple.

Why a Plug-in?

There are typical patterns or signs you notice when writing code that are worthwhile to abstract into a plug-in. If you find yourself imagining another project or situation in which some code you've written could be reused, that's a good sign that you should turn it into a plug-in. Your accordion code is a perfect example of this.

If you find yourself writing very similar code multiple times on different projects, it is a great sign that you should spend time producing a plug-in that can then be easily reused with little effort.

If you find yourself writing code to build a simple accordion more than once, it's time to stop and build a plug-in. It might take a bit longer initially, but afterward you've got a nice, self-contained plug-in that you will never have to write again. Write once, benefit multiple times.

So far, we've spoken about plug-ins in the context of an accordion, but plug-ins can really be made for anything you find yourself doing a lot. It could be a small, three-line plug-in simply to make a certain action much easier, or it could be as large as a complicated image slider.

Your First jQuery Plug-in

Your first jQuery plug-in is going to be incredibly simple. It's just going to log out the value of the ID attribute for every element it's called on.

Before writing a plug-in, it is useful to imagine how another developer will use your plug-in. In this case, imagine doing the following:

```
$("div").logId();
```

© Jack Franklin, Russ Ferguson 2017

J. Franklin, R. Ferguson, *Beginning jQuery*, https://doi.org/10.1007/978-1-4842-3027-5_9

You should be able to open your browser console and see one log statement for every element that $("div") returned. The log should simply be the element's ID attribute, or blank if the element does not have one.

The best way to see how to create this is to dive in and start writing code, with explanations as you go. So, create a new directory, perhaps called logid-plug-in or similar, and put some files in it. First, create index.html:

```
<!DOCTYPE html>
<html>
  <head>
    <title>Chapter 09, Exercise 01</title>
    <script src="jquery.js"></script>
    <script src="logid.jquery.js"></script>
    <script src="app.js"></script>
  </head>
  <body>
    <div id="div1">Hello</div>
    <div id="div2">Hello</div>
    <div id="div3">Hello</div>
    <div id="div4">Hello</div>
    <div id="div5">Hello</div>
    <div id="div6">Hello</div>
    <div id="div7">Hello</div>
  </body>
</html>
```

Put the jQuery source in the directory, too, in a file named jquery.js. Finally, create two more blank files. The first should be called logid.jquery.js, which will house your plug-in, and the second app.js, where you'll write the code that utilizes the plug-in. It's convention to name your plug-in file name.jquery.js, so you'll stick to that.

We'll show you the implementation of the plug-in, and then explain it in detail. Here's the entirety of the code to get your logId plug-in, which you should put into logid.jquery.js:

```
$.fn.logId = function() {
  return this.each(function() {
    console.log(this.id);
  });
};
```

And here's what you should put into app.js to test it out:

```
$(function() {
  $("div").logId();
});
```

And the result in your console should look like Figure 9-1.

div1	logid.jquery.js:3
div2	logid.jquery.js:3
div3	logid.jquery.js:3
div4	logid.jquery.js:3
div5	logid.jquery.js:3
div6	logid.jquery.js:3
div7	logid.jquery.js:3

Figure 9-1. The output from using the plug-in (on the Chrome developer console)

Take a step back to figure out exactly what happened here. The first line adds your method, logId, to jQuery. This is also referred to as *extending* jQuery:

```
$.fn.logId = function() {...});
```

Adding a method to the $.fn method means it's available to be used on a jQuery object. Remember, a jQuery object is the result of running $("div") or similar. All this line does is add a new property to $.fn, logId, which is equal to a function.

The next piece of interest is the each() method:

```
return this.each(function() {...});
```

Within the function, the value of this is the jQuery object your function was called on. So when you call $("div").logId(), the value of this refers to the jQuery object containing the result of $("div"), which will contain all the divs on the page. Therefore, you want to loop over every element within this, so you can run your code on every element.

The other important thing to note is the fact that you return the result of the loop. When looping over something, the initial "thing" will always be returned. So when you run:

```
return this.each(function() {...});
```

At the end of it, this is returned. This means your plug-in is *chainable*, or that someone could call another method after yours, such as:

```
$("div").logId().fadeOut();
```

Unless your plug-in is specifically designed to return a particular value, it should always be chainable. People will assume your plug-in is chainable—and they will get mighty confused if it's not. There's really no excuse not to make it chainable.

Finally, within the loop, the value of this refers to the individual DOM element you are looping over. Note that this is *not* a jQuery object, but just the DOM element. If you wanted to call jQuery methods on it, you'd have to run $(this) first.

All you need to do within the loop is get the element's ID. You could do the following:

```
$(this).attr("id");
```

But in actual fact, it's easy to get at the ID of a DOM element without needing jQuery:

```
this.id
```

That achieves the same thing and is leaner than the jQuery equivalent, so there's no reason not to. So, you now have the following:

```
$.fn.logId = function() {
  return this.each(function() {
    console.log(this.id);
  });
};
```

Congratulations! You've just written your first jQuery plug-in!

Improvements

There are still a few issues with this plug-in, though. The first to tackle is the problem with how you define your plug-in. Currently it's done like so:

```
$.fn.logId = function() {...});
```

However, there is no guarantee that the $ variable refers to jQuery. Sometimes people who use jQuery will not allow it to use the $ variable because another script or plug-in might be using it. Granted, this is fairly unlikely, but you should never assume that $ is jQuery. It's easy enough to get jQuery to release $, through its noConflict() method (http://api.jquery.com/jQuery.noConflict/). Here's an example:

```
jQuery.noConflict();
// now, $ is reset to whatever it was before jQuery was loaded

jQuery("div");
```

jQuery exists as two global variables by default: $ and jQuery. They both are identical, so if jQuery.noConflict() is called, you can still use jQuery through the jQuery method, but not through $.

To be safe, you should use the jQuery variable rather than $ within your plug-in:

```
jQuery.fn.logId = function() {
  return this.each(function() {
    console.log(this.id);
  });
};
```

But typing jQuery instead of $ is irritating. Thankfully, there's a better way to do things.

One way to do it would be to create a function that defines your function. The very first thing you do is set $ equal to jQuery:

```
var definePlugin = function() {
  var $ = jQuery;
  $.fn.logId = function() {
    return this.each(function() {
      console.log(this.id);
    });
  };
};

definePlugin();
```

This works because variables defined within a function are only available within that function, so you can safely define $ without defining it globally. You may not like this solution though, even though it works. Defining and then calling a function seems like a long-winded way of doing things. If only there was a way of defining and then immediately executing a function...

Immediately-Invoked Function Expressions

The term "Immediately-Invoked Function Expression" (IIFE) was coined by prolific JavaScript developer Ben Alman on his personal blog, in an article about functions that are defined and then immediately invoked (http://benalman.com/news/2010/11/immediately-invoked-function-expression/). The article is a great read but goes into a lot of depth, so you may want to read it once you're more comfortable with jQuery and wish to learn more about the specifics of JavaScript.

An *IIFE* is a function that is immediately defined and then executed. Try loading your JS console in a browser and then running this line of code:

```
(function() { console.log("hey"); })();
```

What you will see is the word "hey" logged right back at you. You just defined a function—albeit an anonymous one (you never gave it a name)—and executed it, all in the same line. The key here, as you might have guessed, is the pair of parentheses at the end of the line and the pair around the function definition.

The brackets around the function are due to how JavaScript's parser works. If you try:

```
function() { console.log("hey"); }
```

you will get a syntax error:

```
SyntaxError: Unexpected token (
```

This is the syntax error Google Chrome provides; each browser does it slightly different. Firefox, for example, will state "SyntaxError: function statement requires a name." This is because the parser thinks you're defining a new function, and as such is expecting a name between the function keyword and the opening bracket. It thinks you are *declaring* a function. Hence, this doesn't work because you'll get the same error:

```
function() { console.log("hey"); }()
```

Wrapping it in parentheses tells the parser that it's an *expression* rather than a *declaration*, meaning that it doesn't expect a name and parses the line as a function expression; in other words, it evaluates the contents of the function. The second, empty pair of parentheses simply calls your newly defined function.

So what does this all have to do with the initial problem? Well, IIFEs can take parameters, too. Try this in your console:

```
(function(x) { console.log(x); })("hey");
```

Here you define a function that takes one argument, x, and logs it. When you call it, you then pass in that value. It's no different than doing this:

```
function log(x) {
  console.log(x);
};
log("hey");
```

Now that you know you can do that, you should be able to see how it applies to the initial issue. You can define the function, immediately execute it, and pass in jQuery much more succinctly:

```
(function($) {
  // our plugin here
})(jQuery);
```

Within that function, you can use $ as jQuery, regardless of whether it is defined as jQuery outside the function . With that, your plug-in becomes much more robust:

```
(function($) {
  $.fn.logId = function() {
    return this.each(function() {
      console.log(this.id);
    });
  };
})(jQuery);
```

■ **Note**   IIFEs are one of the most complex parts of JavaScript used in this book. If you're comfortable with them after this, you're doing really well. Don't worry if you need to read this section more than once; the way IIFEs work is not immediately straightforward. If you'd like more information, the best resource is Ben Alman's IIFE article at `http://benalman.com/news/2010/11/immediately-invoked-function-expression/`.

Giving the User Options

When making a plug-in, it might be beneficial to let the user choose how it acts in a certain spot. You might let the user choose the text color or, if your plug-in animates DOM elements, how quickly to animate something.

You are now going to create another small plug-in similar to your first. It will be a function for logging to the console, but for logging any attribute. So you'll need to let the user pass in the attribute they want to be logged.

Create a new directory, perhaps `logattribute-plug-in`, and create a new `index.html` file with the following code. It is identical to the HTML in the previous plug-in you made, except the file name of your plug-in is different.

```
<!DOCTYPE html>
<html>
  <head>
    <title>Chapter 09, Exercise 02</title>
    <script src="jquery.js"></script>
    <script src="logattr.jquery.js"></script>
    <script src="app.js"></script>
  </head>
  <body>
    <div id="div1">Hello</div>
    <div id="div2">Hello</div>
    <div id="div3">Hello</div>
    <div id="div4">Hello</div>
```

```
    <div id="div5">Hello</div>
    <div id="div6">Hello</div>
    <div id="div7">Hello</div>
  </body>
</html>
```

Create a blank app.js file and a logattr.jquery.js file, which should contain the following code, the basis for your plug-in:

```
(function($) {
  $.fn.logAttr = function() {
  };
})(jQuery);
```

You're using an IIFE once more around your plug-in code, which is something you'll do for all plug-ins from now on.

Take a first stab at implementing the following:

```
 (function($) {
  $.fn.logAttr = function(attr) {
    return this.each(function() {
      console.log($(this).attr(attr));
    });
  };
})(jQuery);
```

You simply define a function that takes an attribute as an argument, and then use the attr() method within the loop to log it out. To test it out, place this code into app.js and then load index.html in the browser:

```
$(function() {
  $("div").logAttr("id");
});
```

If you check out the console, you'll see each div's ID logged.

Let's say you're building this for a client, who comes back with the following requests:

- They would like to be able to define a backup value to log if the element doesn't have the attribute specified.

- They would like to be able to switch between using the console and simply alerting variables, because some browsers they need to test in do not have a console.

These are both reasonable requests. Sort out the backup value first. It would make sense for it to be another parameter, so add it. Then, you can log out the attribute if it exists, and if not, the backup value. Let's use the following:

```
(function($) {
  $.fn.logAttr = function(attr, backup) {
    return this.each(function() {
      console.log($(this).attr(attr) || backup);
    });
  };
})(jQuery);
```

133

This is the key line:

```
console.log($(this).attr(attr) || backup);
```

It works because if the element doesn't have the attribute, undefined is returned. Then, the statement becomes

```
undefined || backup
```

undefined is evaluated to false, so then backup is evaluated and returned.

To test this, add a rel attribute to one of the divs:

```
<div id="div1" rel="someDiv">Hello</div>
```

And then change the contents of app.js to

```
$(function() {
  $("div").logAttr("rel", "N/A");
});
```

When you run that in the browser, you'll see "someDiv" logged once, and "N/A" logged six times.

Next, add another option to the plug-in, which if set to true, will use alert instead of console.log:

```
(function($) {
  $.fn.logAttr = function(attr, backup, useAlert) {
    return this.each(function() {
      if(useAlert) {
        alert($(this).attr(attr) || backup);
      } else {
        console.log($(this).attr(attr) || backup);
      }
    });
  };
})(jQuery);
```

And it's used by simply adding true as the third argument when you call the plug-in:

```
$(function() {
  $("div").logAttr("rel", "N/A", true);
});
```

This is starting to get messy, however. A better option would be to let the end user pass in an object of key-value pairs that are the options you want. You'll do that shortly. First, there's a bit of refactoring you can do:

```
if(useAlert) {
  alert($(this).attr(attr) || backup);
} else {
  console.log($(this).attr(attr) || backup);
}
```

Here you are repeating $(this).attr(attr) || backup twice. Better to save that to a variable:

```
var val = $(this).attr(attr) || backup;
if(useAlert) {
  alert(val);
} else {
  console.log(val);
}
```

However, this can be further shortened with the ternary operator:

```
var val = $(this).attr(attr) || backup;
useAlert ? alert(val) : console.log(val);
```

That's a much nicer implementation.

Adding Options to Your Plug-ins

We don't like the way that the user configures the plug-in. In our opinion, the following is messy:

```
$.fn.logAttr = function(attr, backup, useAlert)
```

If users want to set useAlert to true, but leave the backup as its default (which is undefined), they'd have to call the plug-in like this:

```
$("div").logAttr("rel", undefined, true);
```

And that is incredibly messy. You should only make users specify options when they don't want to use the default values. That's where using an object to store the options is beneficial. So instead, you can have users call the plug-in like so:

```
$("div").logAttr({
  attr: "rel",
  useAlert: true
});
```

This is the next thing you'll do in this chapter, before finishing your logAttr plug-in and looking at the accordion plug-in using the code that you wrote earlier.

In terms of implementing the ability to pass in an object, there are three steps:

- Create an object containing the options, set to the default values.

- Allow the user to pass in an object containing the desired settings.

- Overwrite your defaults with the user's options.

The first two steps are very easy. First, change the function so that it takes one argument, the options object:

```
$.fn.logAttr = function(opts) {
```

And then, within that function, define the defaults:

```
var defaults = {
  attr: "id",
  backup: "N/A",
  useAlert: false
};
```

The next part is to take the defaults and overwrite them with the options the user passed in. This is such a common thing for plug-ins to do that jQuery provides a utility method called $.extend (http://api. jquery.com/jQuery.extend/) to do it. It has a few use cases, but the main one for your use is that it can take two objects and merge them into one object. If a property is defined in both objects, the later object takes precedence. Take these two objects, for example:

```
var objectOne = { x: 2, y: 3, z: 4 };
var objectTwo = { x: 4, a: 5 };
```

Then call $.extend, passing in these objects:

```
$.extend(objectOne, objectTwo);
```

This will take objectTwo and merge it into objectOne, modifying it to contain the results of merging the objects. In this case, objectOne would look like this:

```
{ x: 4, y: 3, z: 4, a: 5 }
```

Notice that because x existed in objectTwo, it was used over the x that existed within objectOne.

Typically, you will not want to modify either of the objects, but instead create a new object from the result of merging. This can be achieved by passing in a blank object to $.extend as the first argument. The return value of $.extend is always the merged object.

```
var objectOne = { x: 2, y: 3, z: 4 };
var objectTwo = { x: 4, a: 5 };

var merged = $.extend({}, objectOne, objectTwo);
```

This leaves you a new object, merged, that contains:

```
{ x: 4, y: 3, z: 4, a: 5 }
```

However, objectOne and objectTwo have not been altered. It's this usage that you use in your plug-ins. Implementing this into your plug-in, you end up with the following:

```
(function($) {
  $.fn.logAttr = function(opts) {
    var defaults = {
      attr: "id",
      backup: "N/A",
      useAlert: false
    };
    var options = $.extend({}, defaults, opts);
    return this.each(function() {
```

```
      var val = $(this).attr(options.attr) || options.backup;
      options.useAlert ? alert(val) : console.log(val);
    });
  };
})(jQuery);
```

After defining the defaults, you then use $.extend to merge opts, the object the user passed in, into defaults, and create a new object. $.extend returns this value, so you store it to options, a new variable.

Previously in your options, you referred to the user options as attr or backup; now they exist within options, so they have to be referred to as options.attr and options.backup.

Now the usage of your plug-in has changed, so head into app.js and update it:

```
$(function() {
  $("div").logAttr({
    attr: "rel"
  });
});
```

The beauty of using an option should now be apparent. It's so much clearer as to which options you're setting because you set them through a key/value pairs object. Also, you only have to specify the ones that you want different from the default.

Now that you've made a slightly more complicated function, it's time to revisit the code for the accordion you wrote back in Chapter 5 and turn that into a plug-in.

The Accordion Plug-in

Let's revisit the code you wrote for your accordion. You could either create a new directory or copy the previous one. Here are the contents of app.js:

```
$(function() {
  var accordion = $("#accordion");
  var headings = $("h2");
  var paragraphs = $("p");

  var animateAccordion = function(elem, duration, easing) {
    paragraphs.stop(true, true).slideUp(duration, easing);
    $(elem).stop(true, true).slideDown(duration, easing);
  }

  paragraphs.not(":first").hide();
  accordion.on("click", "h2", function() {
    var t = $(this);
    var tPara = t.next();
    if(!tPara.is(":visible")) {
      tPara.trigger("showParagraph");
    }
  });

  accordion.on("showParagraph", "p", function() {
    animateAccordion(this, 600, "easeInCirc");
  });
});
```

And here's the HTML from index.html:

```html
<!DOCTYPE html>
<html>
  <head>
    <title>Chapter 09, Accordion Plugin</title>
    <script src="jquery.js"></script>
    <script src="app.js"></script>
    <link rel="stylesheet" type="text/css" href="style.css" />
  </head>
  <body>
    <div id="accordion">
      <h2>Heading</h2>
      <p>Lorem ipsum dolor sit amet, consectetur adipisicing elit, sed do eiusmod tempor
      incididunt ut labore et dolore magna aliqua. Ut enim ad minim veniam, quis nostrud
      exercitation ullamco laboris nisi ut aliquip ex ea commodo consequat. Duis aute irure
      dolor in reprehenderit in voluptate velit esse cillum dolore eu fugiat nulla pariatur.
      Excepteur sint occaecat cupidatat non proident, sunt in culpa qui officia deserunt
      mollit anim id est laborum.</p>
      <h2>Heading 2</h2>
      <p>Lorem ipsum dolor sit amet, consectetur adipisicing elit, sed do eiusmod tempor
      incididunt ut labore et dolore magna aliqua. Ut enim ad minim veniam, quis nostrud
      exercitation ullamco laboris nisi ut aliquip ex ea commodo consequat. Duis aute irure
      dolor in reprehenderit in voluptate velit esse cillum dolore eu fugiat nulla pariatur.
      Excepteur sint occaecat cupidatat non proident, sunt in culpa qui officia deserunt
      mollit anim id est laborum.</p>
      <h2>Heading 3</h2>
      <p>Lorem ipsum dolor sit amet, consectetur adipisicing elit, sed do eiusmod tempor
      incididunt ut labore et dolore magna aliqua. Ut enim ad minim veniam, quis nostrud
      exercitation ullamco laboris nisi ut aliquip ex ea commodo consequat. Duis aute irure
      dolor in reprehenderit in voluptate velit esse cillum dolore eu fugiat nulla pariatur.
      Excepteur sint occaecat cupidatat non proident, sunt in culpa qui officia deserunt
      mollit anim id est laborum.</p>
    </div>
  </body>
</html>
```

You also had a small amount of CSS in style.css:

```css
#accordion {
  width: 500px;
  border: 1px solid black;
}

#accordion h2 {
  padding: 5px;
  margin: 0;
  background: #ddd;
}

#accordion p {
  padding: 0 5px;
}
```

In the original accordion, you also included the jQuery UI source, so you could use different easing types. You're not going to include that this time; just simply use the default animation.

Start work on turning it into a plug-in. A likely use for the plug-in is to call it on the div that contains all the content. You then have to pass it the element types that are used for the headings and content. For example, you might call it like so:

```
$("#accordion").accordion({
  headings: "h2",
  content: "p"
});
```

Create a new file, accordion.jquery.js, and leave it blank. If you like, you might load up your old accordion code to use as a reference. Alter app.js so that it uses your plug-in:

```
$(function() {
  $("#accordion").accordion({
    headings: "h2",
    content: "p"
  });
});
```

Obviously, this won't work right now, but your task now is to get it working. You should also edit index. html, adding in the new accordion.jquery.js file before app.js:

```
<script src="jquery.js"></script>
<script src="accordion.jquery.js"></script>
<script src="app.js"></script>
```

Now you can get started. At the top of the plug-in file (accordion.jquery.js), write the initial template:

```
(function($) {

  $.fn.accordion = function(opts) {
    var defaults = {
      headings: "h2",
      content: "p"
    };
    var options = $.extend({}, defaults, opts);
  };

})(jQuery);
```

Here you use an IIFE to make certain that you can use $ and that it refers to jQuery. Create the function, which will take one argument—an object of options—before setting up the default options. You may need more options; if you do, you can add them as you go. Then, create the final set of objects, merging the user's options with the defaults.

Next, you set up the loop that will contain your functionality. This loops over every element the plug-in was called on. Remember, you return it so that your plug-in is chainable. Within the loop, you can get at the current element through this, and so create a $this variable, which refers to $(this), which is the current element wrapped in the jQuery object. If you're working on a project with lots of variables, some of which refer to jQuery objects and others that don't, consider prefixing the ones that do with a $ as a visual note to yourself that those variables are jQuery objects.

```
return this.each(function() {
  var $this = $(this);
});
```

You then need to store references to the headings and content. In your initial accordion, you did the following:

```
var headings = $("h2");
var paragraphs = $("p");
```

But in this case, the selectors are defined within the options. You should also limit your search to within the accordion:

```
return this.each(function() {
  var $this = $(this);
  var headings = $this.children(options.headings);
  var paragraphs = $this.children(options.content);
});
```

If you look at the initial accordion, you had a small utility function, `animateAccordion()`, which did the animations for you:

```
var animateAccordion = function(elem, duration, easing) {
  paragraphs.stop(true, true).slideUp(duration, easing);
  $(elem).stop(true, true).slideDown(duration, easing);
}
```

You're going to keep this function, but with one difference. Because you are no longer allowing the easing to be customized, and are sticking with the default, remove that option. Your plug-in loop should now look like this:

```
return this.each(function() {
  var $this = $(this);
  var headings = $this.children(options.headings);
  var paragraphs = $this.children(options.content);

  var animateAccordion = function(elem, duration) {
    paragraphs.stop(true, true).slideUp(duration);
    $(elem).stop(true, true).slideDown(duration);
  };
});
```

Your next piece of code does the animations. It needs very little changing. This is it for now:

```
paragraphs.not(":first").hide();
accordion.on("click", "h2", function() {
  var t = $(this);
  var tPara = t.next();
  if(!tPara.is(":visible")) {
    tPara.trigger("showParagraph");
  }
});
```

```
accordion.on("showParagraph", "p", function() {
  animateAccordion(this, 600, "easeInCirc");
});
```

There are only a couple of pieces to change. First, instead of referring to the variable `accordion`, you now refer to $this. Second, both of the calls refer to the headings and contents through `"h2"` or `"p"`. You need to use the `options.headings` and `options.content` variables instead. Finally, remove the third parameter from the `animateAccordion()` argument because you are no longer supporting different easing methods.

That leaves the code looking like so:

```
paragraphs.not(":first").hide();
$this.on("click", options.headings, function() {
  var t = $(this);
  var tPara = t.next();
  if(!tPara.is(":visible")) {
   tPara.trigger("showParagraph");
  }
});

$this.on("showParagraph", options.content, function() {
  animateAccordion(this, 600);
});
```

And you are now done. Put that within the loop in your plug-in, and your accordion is complete! `accordion.jquery.js` should now look like this:

```
(function($) {

  $.fn.accordion = function(opts) {
    var defaults = {
      headings: "h2",
      content: "p"
    };

    var options = $.extend({}, defaults, opts);

    return this.each(function() {
      var $this = $(this);
      var headings = $this.children(options.headings);
      var paragraphs = $this.children(options.content);

      var animateAccordion = function(elem, duration) {
        paragraphs.stop(true, true).slideUp(duration);
        $(elem).stop(true, true).slideDown(duration);
      };

      paragraphs.not(":first").hide();
      $this.on("click", options.headings, function() {
        var t = $(this);
        var tPara = t.next();
```

```
      if(!tPara.is(":visible")) {
        tPara.trigger("showParagraph");
      }
    });

    $this.on("showParagraph", options.content, function() {
      animateAccordion(this, 600);
    });
  });
};

})(jQuery);
```

If you load index.html in a browser, you should see it all working as before. Congratulations on your first "proper" jQuery plug-in! You could make some improvements, though. The first is providing support for callbacks.

Adding Callback Support

When you explored animations in Chapter 7, you discovered the beauty of callbacks and the ability to run some code. It would be fantastic if you could allow anyone using your plug-in to define a callback that would be run once an animation happened, which meant that the user switched to a new section.

You might think adding callback functionality is complicated, but it's really not. The first thing to do is add a new option to your defaults, defining what the default callback function should be. If the user doesn't define one, then presumably she doesn't want anything to run once the animation is done, so the default should simply be a function that does nothing:

```
var defaults = {
  headings: "h2",
  content: "p",
  callback: function() {}
};
```

Next, you need to edit your animateAccordion() function to take a callback. It should take it as an argument and pass it straight through to the animations. However, you should only pass it through to one of them. If you were to pass it through to both the slideUp() and slideDown() functions, you would have it called twice. Both animations run for the same amount of time, so they both finish at the same time. This means you can add it to only one of the animations:

```
var animateAccordion = function(elem, duration, callback) {
  paragraphs.stop(true, true).slideUp(duration);
  $(elem).stop(true, true).slideDown(duration, callback);
};
```

Finally, you need to edit the call to animateAccordion() to pass through the callback:

```
$this.on("showParagraph", options.content, function() {
  animateAccordion(this, 600, options.callback);
});
```

Note that `options.callback` is simply a reference to the function. `options.callback()` would execute the function, which is not what you want. Referring to a function without parentheses means you get a reference to the function and it does not execute. Let's test this out. Edit your `app.js` file so that you pass in a callback:

```
$(function() {
  $("#accordion").accordion({
    headings: "h2",
    content: "p",
    callback: function() {
      alert("changed");
    }
  });
});
```

Now, whenever anything slides down within the accordion, you'll get an alert.

The final tweak you'll make is to allow the user to set the duration. For any plug-ins that include animations, it's important to let the user change the speed. This is very easy to do. Add the default:

```
var defaults = {
  headings: "h2",
  content: "p",
  callback: function() {},
  duration: 600
};
```

And again, it's just a case of editing the call to `animateAccordion()`:

```
$this.on("showParagraph", options.content, function() {
  animateAccordion(this, options.duration, options.callback);
});
```

And with that, your accordion plug-in is done. Here's the final code:

```
(function($) {

  $.fn.accordion = function(opts) {
    var defaults = {
      headings: "h2",
      content: "p",
      callback: function() {},
      duration: 600
    };

    var options = $.extend({}, defaults, opts);

    return this.each(function() {
      var $this = $(this);
      var headings = $this.children(options.headings);
      var paragraphs = $this.children(options.content);
```

```
    var animateAccordion = function(elem, duration, callback) {
      paragraphs.stop(true, true).slideUp(duration);
      $(elem).stop(true, true).slideDown(duration, callback);
    };

    paragraphs.not(":first").hide();
    $this.on("click", options.headings, function() {
      var t = $(this);
      var tPara = t.next();
      if(!tPara.is(":visible")) {
        tPara.trigger("showParagraph");
      }
    });

    $this.on("showParagraph", options.content, function() {
      animateAccordion(this, options.duration, options.callback);
    });
  });
};

})(jQuery);
```

You can then use this option to set the animation, like so:

```
$(function() {
  $("#accordion").accordion({
    duration: 10000
  });
});
```

Summary

Don't underestimate the power of plug-ins. You now have a simple accordion that you could use in any project. That's the real benefit: plug-ins give you modular, portable code that you can pick up and reuse as needed. In the next chapter, you'll increase complexity and write a plug-in for API usage. We'll then talk briefly about distributing your plug-ins, including minifying your source code and writing good documentation.

CHAPTER 10

■ ■ ■

More jQuery Plug-ins

You ended the last chapter with a pretty awesome accordion plug-in that you built based on the initial accordion code you wrote in Chapter 5. In this chapter, you will take your TVmaze API work from Chapter 8 and turn it into a plug-in. You'll do this by making a slightly different type of plug-in, one that exists directly on the jQuery object. This means instead of calling it on a set, as you did previously:

```
$("div").somePlugin();
```

you call it directly:

```
$.somePlugin();
```

There are certain situations in which you should use the first style, and other situations where you should use the latter. This chapter explains the latter. There are a few other things to cover in this chapter:

- You'll further explore ways to make your plug-in more useful. Keeping it generic and making sure it does the job it is supposed to do makes it easier for others to use. You'll look at techniques for doing this.

- We'll briefly discuss best practices for documenting your plug-in and show examples.

The TVmaze API Plug-in

To refresh your memory, here's the code you wrote for grabbing the list of episodes for a show including the use of the dataType property that we used in Chapter 7:

```
$(function() {
  var req = $.ajax({
    url: " http://api.tvmaze.com/shows/396/episodes ",
    dataType: "jsonp"
  });
  req.done(function(data) {
    console.log(data);
  });
});
```

© Jack Franklin, Russ Ferguson 2017
J. Franklin, R. Ferguson, *Beginning jQuery*, https://doi.org/10.1007/978-1-4842-3027-5_10

It's time to turn this code into a jQuery plug-in. It is going to exist directly on the jQuery object because you're going to extend your plug-in to have two distinct methods. One will get the data for a single show, and the other will get all the episodes from the show and construct a list of them. The goal is to be able to call them like so:

```
$.tvmaze.getShow();
$.tvmaze.getEpisodes();
```

So your plug-in will exist on the jQuery object, but contain more than one method to be called.

First, create a new directory for this project. If you remember using npm before, here is a good opportunity to use it again. If you have not installed http-server, make sure Node.js has already been installed, then at the command line type npm install -g http-server. After that, also using the command line, type http-server. This will make your current directory a local web server.

You can see everything that you are working on in your browser by typing localhost:8080.

First you will create the basic structure of the page. To make it look nice, you will also include Twitter Bootstrap (http://getbootstrap.com). Create blank app.js and tvmaze.jquery.js files, and an index.html here we add the parts that we need to style the page using Bootstrap (refer to http://getbootstrap.com for instructions on how to use Bootstrap from the CDN):

```html
<!DOCTYPE html>
<html>
  <head>
    <title>Chapter 10, TVMaze Plugin</title>
    <link rel='stylesheet' href='add URL to bootstrap css'>
</head>
  <body>
        <div class="container">
                <h1> TV Maze - TV Show Search </h1>
                    <form>
        <div class="form-group">
          <input type="text" class="form-control" id="showInput" placeholder="Search TV
          Show" required>
<button tyhpe="submit" class=" btn btn-primary" id-"submitButton">Submit</button>
        </dir>
                </form>
           </div>
     <div>
           <table class="table">
                   <thead id="tableHead">
                        <tr>
                            <td>Name</td>
                            <td>Network</td>
                          <td>Type</td>
                            <td>Image</td>
                        </tr>
                   </thead>
             <tbody id="tableBody">
                </tbody>
           </table>
```

```
    <table class="table">
        <thead>
            <tr>
                <td>Airdate</td>
                <td>Episode Name</td>
                <td>Episode Number</td>
                <td>Season</td>
                <td>Run Time</td>
                <td>Summary</td>
            </tr>
        </thead>
        <tbody id="episodeInfo">

        </tbody>
    </table>
  </div>
</div>
  <script src="jquery.js"></script>
  <script src="tvmaze.jquery.js"></script>
  <script src="app.js"></script>
 </body>
</html>
```

At this point your page should look something like Figure 10-1.

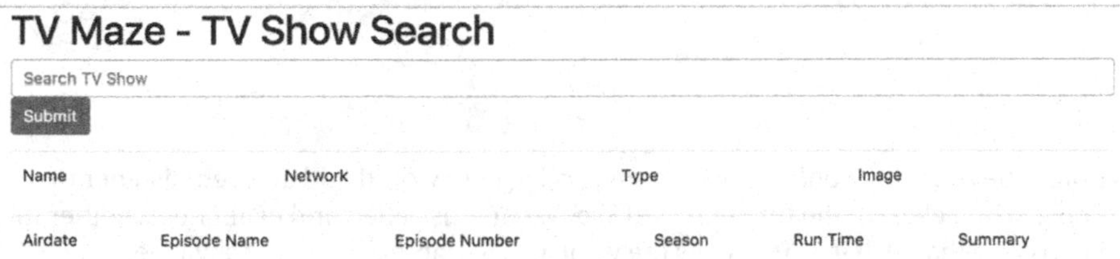

TV Maze - TV Show Search

Search TV Show

Submit

Name	Network	Type	Image

Airdate	Episode Name	Episode Number	Season	Run Time	Summary

Figure 10-1. *The page with some basic CSS styling*

Open tvmaze.jquery.js and add the following. We add the following to create the tvmaze object and assign methods to it:

```
(function($) {

$.tvmaze = {
    getEpisode: function(showId, callback) {
    var req = $.ajax({
    url:'http://api.tvmaze.com/shows/' + showId + '/episodes'
    });
                req.done(callBack);
    },
```

```
    getShow: function(showName, callBack) {
        var req = $.ajax({
                url:'http://api.tvmaze.com/search/shows/?q=' + showName
            });

            req.done(callBack);
    }
};

})(jQuery);
```

With the plug-in now in place, you can start to make calls to TVmaze. Over time, you can add features to make other API calls. For now, you can open app.js and start to get the application to work. Similar to the TVmaze plug-in, this is going to be an IIFE (Immediately-Invoked Function Expression). In short, it will run as soon as it has been created.

```
(function() {
        $('#submitButton').on ('click', getShowName);

        function getShowName(evt){
                evt.proventDefault();
                if($('#showInput')[0].valuie.length > 0){
            let searchValue = $('#showInput')[0].value;
        $().tvmaze.getShow(searchValue, (results) => {
            displayShowResults(results[0].show);
                    });
    }
        }
})();
```

At this point, the function would have executed and jQuery would add an event listener to "submitButton". When clicked, the function "getShowName()" is called and evaluates whether the value of the text field is greater than 0. If it is, it assigns the value to a variable called searchValue.

Here is where you get to use your recently created plug-in. The method getShow() is called with the value passed from the text field. In this example, you may notice that the callback function looks a little different. This example is using an arrow function. For your purposes, it works exactly the same as a normal anonymous function. Your result returns an array of objects that then get passed off to the displayShowResults() function, which you add next as follows:

■ **Note** For more information on how arrow functions are different than function expressions, look at the MDN Web Docs: https://developer.mozilla.org/en-US/docs/Web/JavaScript/Reference/Functions/Arrow_functions

---

```
function displayShowResults(results){
    $('#tableBody').html('<td id="episodeName" data-episodeid="' + results.id + '">'
        + result.name + '</td>' + '<td>'
        + checkNetwork(results.network) + '</td>'
        + '<td>' + results.type + '</td>'
```

```
        + '<td> <img class="image-border" src=" '
        + results.image.medium '"> </td>');
    $('#episodeInfo tr').remove();

      $('#episodeName').on('click', (event) => {
            getEpisodes(event.target.dataset.episodeid);
      });
}

function checkNetwork(networkName)
  if(networkName != null)  {
      return networkName.name;
    }else{
        return 'Not Listed';
    }
}
```

Here you start to display the results of the API call your plug-in made for you. jQuery adds a row with the results, displaying the ID, name, and image. There is also a function called checkNetwork( ), which is included only in the case of the result returning from the API is null. In that instance, you would get an error. To avoid that, you can check if there is a null value and, if there is, just return the string 'Not Listed'.

The next line removes any previous listing of TV episodes. The first time it runs, there will be nothing to remove, but you will see shortly how this becomes important. Another click event is added to the ID episodeName.

If you were wondering what the data attribute is doing, here is where it comes in. The data attribute is part of HTML5 and allows you to add extra information that does not have any visual representation. When retrieving the information, you can look at the dataset property and call your custom-made property episodeid. With this intact, you can now make another call to the TVmaze plug-in and get all the episodes for that TV show:

```
function getEpisodes(episodeID){
        $().tvmaze.getEpisodes(episodeID, function(results){
          for(var I = 0; I < results.length; i++){
              $('#episodeInfo').append('<tr> <td>'
                    + results[i].airdate + '</td> <td>'
                    + results[i].name + '</td> <td>'
                    + results[i].number + '</td> <td>'
                    + results[i].season + '</td> <td>'
                    + results[i].runtime + '</td> <td>'
                    + results[i].summary + '<td>'
                    + '</tr>')
          }
        });
}
```

The last function in this example calls the TVmaze plug-in. When the results are returned, it will loop over them and append a new row to the existing table with information about the episodes.

If you are running this on your local web server (for example, http-server), you should be able to make calls to the API and get results back. Figure 10-2 shows a partial screenshot of what that should look like.

TV Maze – TV Show Search

Star Wars: Rebels

Submit

Name	Network	Type	Image
Star Wars Rebels	Disney XD	Animation	

Airdate	Episode Name	Episode Number	Season	Run Time	Summary
2014-10-03	Spark of Rebellion	0	1	60	Ezra Bridger is an orphan on Lothal, an Outer Rim world. He interferes with the *Ghost* crew's theft of blaster rifles from the Empire. Ezra is shanghaied by the crew while making their getaway. The rifles are sold to buy food and information. The food is given to the displaced people of Lothal, while the information leads the crew to a group of imprisoned Wookiees.

Figure 10-2. Results from the TVmaze site using the jQuery plugin

Documentation

We'd like to very briefly discuss how to document your plug-in. Documenting your plug-in is important for other developers who might use it, but for you as well. When you revisit a plug-in after an extended time, good documentation is really helpful.

You need to document each method clearly. It is a good idea to provide the following details:

- Give a one- or two-sentence description of what the method does.

- Note the options that the method takes in, example values, and the default value for every option that has one.

- Give an example of the plug-in's usage and the data it returns.

The following is an example of how I would document your getShow() method:

THE GETSHOW METHOD

getShow() is a method that takes in a string representing the name of a TV show and makes an Ajax request to TVmaze, returning the JSON data of that show.

- showName: This is a string that is the ID of the TV show you'd like to get the data for; for example: "Gravity Falls"

- callback: A function that will be called when the Ajax request returns the data.

It takes a single string:

Here's an example usage, and the response that's received:

```
$.tvmaze.getShow({
showName:"Star Wars: Rebels",
  callback: function(data) {
    console.log(data);
  }
});
```

And the JSON that is returned:

```
▼ [{score: 40.339504,…}]
 ▼ 0: {score: 40.339504,…}
    score: 40.339504
   ▼ show: {id: 117, url: "http://www.tvmaze.com/shows/117/star-wars-rebels", name: "Star Wars Rebels",…}
    ▶ externals: {tvrage: 35995, thetvdb: 283468, imdb: "tt2930604"}
    ▶ genres: ["Action", "Adventure", "Family", "Science-Fiction"]
      id: 117
    ▶ image: {medium: "http://static.tvmaze.com/uploads/images/medium_portrait/26/66846.jpg",…}
      language: "English"
      name: "Star Wars Rebels"
    ▶ network: {id: 25, name: "Disney XD", country: {name: "United States", code: "US", timezone: "America/New_York"}}
      officialSite: "http://disneyxd.disney.com/star-wars-rebels"
      premiered: "2014-10-03"
    ▶ rating: {average: 7.7}
      runtime: 30
    ▶ schedule: {time: "11:00", days: ["Saturday"]}
      status: "Running"
      summary: "<p><b>Star Wars Rebels</b>, set five years before the events of Star Wars: Episode IV – A New Hope, tells the story of the Rebe
      type: "Animation"
      updated: 1494809306
      url: "http://www.tvmaze.com/shows/117/star-wars-rebels"
    ▶ webChannel: {id: 123, name: "WATCH Disney XD",…}
      weight: 93
    ▶ _links: {self: {href: "http://api.tvmaze.com/shows/117"},…}
```

That's an example of how I'd document a method. My key rule is that if I'm considering whether or not to document a certain bit of functionality, I do it anyway. It's better to have too much documentation than not enough.

Summary

This was yet another complex chapter in which you explored organizing code and learned how to refactor effectively. The methods the end user of your plug-in will call are all just two lines long, with the main work done in your utility methods.

Next, you'll finish the book with a bang by creating an image slider plug-in. You'll use a combination of everything you learned so far in this book to make a nicely packaged jQuery plug-in that is well structured, offers the user customization through options, and can easily be reused.

CHAPTER 11

■ ■ ■

A jQuery Image Slider

You're going to complete the book by building the famed jQuery plug-in: an image slider. This will pull together a lot of parts from the book that you've so far only studied in isolation. You'll use animations to animate your images and events that let the user click through the slider—and end up with a plug-in that's ready for production. You'll also encounter new functionality that you haven't studied yet. For example, you'll hook up your slider to the keyboard so that the user can press the left or right arrows to navigate. And, you'll further increase the complexity by allowing the user to pause and play the slider, as well as making it automatically animate every 20 seconds. Although you made a slider in Chapter 7, you'll start this new one from scratch.

Plan of Attack

Before embarking on a big project, whether it is a full-scale web site or just a plug-in, you should make a list of the key features you'd like to implement. Here's the list you'll be following in this chapter:

- Allow users to click Forward and Back buttons on the screen to navigate through images.

- Let users use their left and right arrow keys to navigate through the images.

- Make the navigation button loop to the beginning when you reach the end of the slider.

- Make the slideshow run automatically every 20 seconds.

- Reset the slider timer if the user clicks the Next or Back buttons so that it doesn't ever automatically scroll after the user clicks a button.

Let's get started!

Project Setup

You've done this so many times now that you're probably used to it, but you need to make a new project directory with the appropriate subfolders, which should contain the following files (leave them all blank for now):

- `index.html`

- `css/style.css`

- `scripts/app.js`

- `scripts/slider.jquery.js`

© Jack Franklin, Russ Ferguson 2017
J. Franklin, R. Ferguson, *Beginning jQuery*, https://doi.org/10.1007/978-1-4842-3027-5_11

You should also download the latest version of jQuery and save it to jquery.js. If you all ready installed Node.js, then make sure you have http-server installed.

Edit the contents of index.html to look like the following code. This simply loads your JavaScript and CSS files, and sets up the HTML structure that will become the slider.

```
<!DOCTYPE html>
<html>
  <head>
    <title>Chapter 11, Image Slider</title>
    <link rel="stylesheet" href="css/style.css">
    <script src="scripts/jquery.js"></script>
    <script src="scripts/slider.jquery.js"></script>
    <script src="scripts/app.js"></script>
  </head>
  <body>
    <div class="slider">
      <ul>
        <li><img src=" http://placekitten.com/g/300/300 " alt="Kitten" width="300"
        height="300" /></li>
        <li><img src=" http://placekitten.com/g/300/300 " alt="Kitten" width="300"
        height="300" /></li>
        <li><img src=" http://placekitten.com/g/300/300 " alt="Kitten" width="300"
        height="300" /></li>
        <li><img src=" http://placekitten.com/g/300/300 " alt="Kitten" width="300"
        height="300" /></li>
        <li><img src=" http://placekitten.com/g/300/300 " alt="Kitten" width="300"
        height="300" /></li>
        <li><img src=" http://placekitten.com/g/300/300 " alt="Kitten" width="300"
        height="300" /></li>
        <li><img src=" http://placekitten.com/g/300/300 " alt="Kitten" width="300"
        height="300" /></li>
        <li><img src=" http://placekitten.com/g/300/300 " alt="Kitten" width="300"
        height="300" /></li>
        <li><img src=" http://placekitten.com/g/300/300 " alt="Kitten" width="300"
        height="300" /></li>
      </ul>
      <a href="#" class="button back">Back</a>
      <a href="#" class="button forward">Forward</a>
    </div>
  </body>
</html>
```

The CSS that you're going to use is almost identical to the CSS you used for the slider in Chapter 7. It simply makes the unordered list big enough to horizontally accommodate all the pictures, and then makes the div that it sits in only wide enough to show one image. Here we are using images from http://unsplash.com.

```
body {
  padding: 50px;
}
```

```css
.slider {
  width: 300px;
  overflow: hidden;
  height: 400px;
}

.slider ul {
  list-style: none;
  width: 3000px;
  height: 300px;
  margin: 0;
  padding: 0;
}

.slider li {
  float: left;
  width: 300px;
  height: 300px;
}

.button {
  font-family: Arial, sans-serif;
  font-size: 14px;
  display: block;
  padding: 6px;
  border: 1px solid #ccc;
  margin: 10px 0 0 0;
}

.back {
  float: left;
}

.forward {
  float: right;
}

a:link, a:visited {
  color: blue;
  text-decoration: underline;
}

a:hover {
  text-decoration: none;
}
```

With the HTML and CSS in place, run http-server at the command line and you should have something that looks similar to Figure 11-1.

Back   Forward

Figure 11-1. *The styled slider, complete with kittens*

Plug-in Setup

Now open slider.jquery.js in your text editor of choice. Add the following code, which only does the initial setup of your plug-in. It establishes the settings variable by extending the default settings with the ones the user passes in (this is empty right now, but as you continue along, you'll spot places where you should turn a variable into an option). It then enters the loop, which loops over every element that the plug-in was called on, and sets up some initial variables within.

```
function($) {
  $.fn.slider = function(options) {
    var defaults = {};
    var settings = $.extend({}, defaults, options);
    return this.each(function() {
      var $slider = $(this);
      var $sliderList = $slider.children("ul");
      var $sliderItems = $sliderList.children("li");
      var $allButtons = $slider.find(".button");
      var $buttons = {
        forward: $allButtons.filter(".forward"),
        back: $allButtons.filter(".back")
      };
    });
  };
})(jQuery);
```

Notice that this code also stores both buttons within an object. This means you can use $buttons.forward for the Forward button and $buttons.back for the Back button. Putting them in an object as $buttons.forward reads more nicely than having a variable for each. To get at them, you use the filter() method to narrow the set of buttons to contain only the one with a particular class, which is the one you need.

Next, go into your app.js file and add the following:

```
$(function() {
  $(".slider").slider();
});
```

Now you're ready to get started.

Animating the Slider

The slider that you made in Chapter 7 had a utility function for animating the slider. It took three arguments: a direction, a duration, and a callback. Although you won't copy every piece of code directly from the Chapter 7 slider, you will use the utility method:

```
var animateSlider = function(direction, duration, callback) {
  $sliderList.stop(true, true).animate({
    "margin-left" : direction + "=300px"
  }, duration, callback);
};
```

Note one small adjustment: the variable is now called $sliderList, not simply sliderList.

■ **Note**   You'll notice that now we using a mixture of variables, some with a $ at the start ($sliderList), and some without (settings). One way of working with a lot of variables is to give all the variables that reference a jQuery object a $ at the beginning—to allow you to differentiate between them.

Add this method just below the line that sets up the $buttons object. Now it's time to add a click event to the buttons to get the slider working. You can do this in the same way that you did it in Chapter 7. When a button is clicked, check if it's the Back button. If it is, call animateSlider() with "+" as the direction, else call it with "-". This method might seem very simple right now, and it is. It will need refactoring later on.

```
$allButtons.on("click", function(event) {
  var isBackButton = $(this).hasClass("back");
  animateSlider((isBackButton ? "+" : "-"), 1000);
  event.preventDefault();
});
```

The slider works at this point, but with some big pitfalls. You can click the buttons infinitely, meaning that you can scroll past the last image and end up at a blank page. You'll remember you dealt with this in Chapter 7, where you simply disabled the Back/Forward buttons when the slider reached the first/last image. This time, you will handle it a bit differently and make the slider loop continuously, so that clicking the Forward button when you're at the last image will take you back to the first image.

Infinitely Looping

You know that the slider is at the beginning if the margin-left is 0, and you know that the slider is at the end if its left margin is -((numberOfImages -1) * widthOfOneImage). The following are the two small methods to detect if the slider is at the beginning or the end:

```
var isAtBeginning = function() {
  return parseInt($sliderList.css("margin-left"), 10) === 0;
};

var isAtEnd = function() {
  var endMargin = ($sliderItems.length - 1) * $sliderItems.first().children("img").width();
  return parseInt($sliderList.css("margin-left"), 10) === -endMargin;
};
```

Remember, $sliderList.css("margin-left") will give you a string—such as "300px", so use JavaScript's parseInt() to parse the integer, 300, from that. parseInt() takes a second argument, which is the base to use. Here, you can spot that you might be parsing the margin more than once in this slider, so turn that into a new utility method too. This tidies up the code:

```
var getLeftMargin = function() {
  return parseInt($sliderList.css("margin-left"), 10);
};

var isAtBeginning = function() {
  return getLeftMargin() === 0;
};

var isAtEnd = function() {
  var endMargin = ($sliderItems.length - 1) * $sliderItems.first().children("img").width();
  return getLeftMargin() === -endMargin;
};
```

Writing an extra method might seem like it's making your code longer, but it's tidied up the preceding example hugely; plus, it's very likely you will need to use it in other places.

Now that you can detect when the slider is at the beginning or end, you need to get your infinite looping sorted.

If the slider is at the beginning and the Back button is clicked, you need to go all the way to the end. If the slider is at the end and the Forward button is clicked, you need to go all the way to the beginning. The Forward button's behavior is slightly easier because sending the slider back to the beginning is just a matter of setting the left margin to 0.

You can do this in the event handler for the buttons clicked. If the button clicked isn't the Back button, and you are at the end, then you need to loop:

```
$allButtons.on("click", function(event) {
  var isBackButton = $(this).hasClass("back");
  if(!isBackButton && isAtEnd()) {
    // loop to the beginning
  }
  animateSlider((isBackButton ? "+" : "-"), 1000); event.preventDefault();
});
```

To loop, you need to set the slider to have a margin of 0. Because you might need to do this a few times, create another utility method and insert it just below where you define the animateSlider() method:

```
var animateSliderToMargin = function(margin, duration, callback) {
  $sliderList.stop(true, true).animate({
    "margin-left": margin
  }, duration, callback);
};
```

Next you're going to animate this because the animation will make what's happened clearer to the user. The following code shows using the new method in your click handler. Once this change is implemented, you will be able to loop infinitely through the slider going forward.

```
$allButtons.on("click", function(event) {
  var isBackButton = $(this).hasClass("back");
  if(!isBackButton && isAtEnd()) {
    animateSliderToMargin(0, 1000);
  } else {
    animateSlider((isBackButton ? "+" : "-"), 1000);
  }
  event.preventDefault();
});
```

Next, you'll make the Back button work. To do this, you need to set the margin to the maximum negative margin possible. You calculated this earlier when writing your isAtEnd() method:

```
var endMargin = ($sliderItems.length - 1) * $sliderItems.first().children("img").width();
```

Because you'll be using this again, you need to move it into a utility method so that you don't repeat yourself. However, having this in a utility method is overkill. You can simply calculate this variable once, when the slider is initialized, and then reference it later. Just below where you defined the variable $buttons, add the following:

```
var endMargin = ($sliderItems.length - 1) * $sliderItems.first().children("img").width();
```

And now update the isAtEnd() method to simply use that:

```
var isAtEnd = function() {
  return getLeftMargin() === -endMargin;
};
```

You're going to make one more change. Rather than keep endMargin positive and use it as -endMargin when needed, it's much easier to simply make endMargin negative in the first place. Change the variable declaration of endMargin to the following:

```
var endMargin = -(($sliderItems.length - 1) * $sliderItems.first().children("img").width());
```

And now your isAtEnd() method is even simpler:

```
var isAtEnd = function() {
  return getLeftMargin() === endMargin;
};
```

You can now use this in your event handler to make your slider infinitely loop when going backward, as the following demonstrates:

```
$allButtons.on("click", function(event) {
  var isBackButton = $(this).hasClass("back");
  if(!isBackButton && isAtEnd()) {
    animateSliderToMargin(0, 1000);
  } else if(isBackButton && isAtBeginning()) {
    animateSliderToMargin(endMargin, 1000);
  } else {
    animateSlider((isBackButton ? "+" : "-"), 1000);
  }
  event.preventDefault();
});
```

First, check the Forward button and that the user is at the last image on the slider. If so, animate back to the beginning. If not, check if the Back button is clicked and the user is at the beginning of the slider. If so, animate back to the end; otherwise, you just animate backward or forward like normal, because the user is at neither the beginning nor the end.

If you refresh index.html in the browser, you should be able to click the Back button to be taken to the very end of the list. In fact, you should now be able to click back and forward as many times as you like without ever coming to an "end," because your slider loops once you get to the end.

Catch Up

This is a good place to take a breath and see where we are at. The following code shows the full contents of our slider.jquery.js file:

```
(function($) {

  $.fn.slider = function(options) {
    var defaults = {};
    var settings = $.extend({}, defaults, options);

    return this.each(function() {
      // store some initial variables
      var $slider = $(this);
      var $sliderList = $slider.children("ul");
      var $sliderItems = $sliderList.children("li");
      var $allButtons = $slider.find(".button");
      var $buttons = {
        forward: $allButtons.filter(".forward"),
        back: $allButtons.filter(".back")
      };
      var endMargin = -(($sliderItems.length - 1) * $sliderItems.first().children("img").
      width());

      var animateSlider = function(direction, duration, callback) {
        $sliderList.stop(true, true).animate({
          "margin-left" : direction + "=300px"
        }, duration, callback);
      };
```

```
    var animateSliderToMargin = function(margin, duration, callback) {
      $sliderList.stop(true, true).animate({
        "margin-left": margin
      }, duration, callback);
    };

    var getLeftMargin = function() {
      return parseInt($sliderList.css("margin-left"), 10);
    };

    var isAtBeginning = function() {
      return getLeftMargin() === 0;
    };

    var isAtEnd = function() {
      return getLeftMargin() === endMargin;
    };

    $allButtons.on("click", function(event) {
      var isBackButton = $(this).hasClass("back");
      if(!isBackButton && isAtEnd()) {
        animateSliderToMargin(0, 1000);
      } else if(isBackButton && isAtBeginning()) {
        animateSliderToMargin(endMargin, 1000);
      } else {
        animateSlider((isBackButton ? "+" : "-"), 1000);
      }
      event.preventDefault();
    });
  });
};
})(jQuery);
```

Also look at some of the things you could turn into options that the user can pass in. The obvious one is the duration of each animation. You are manually coding the duration to 1000 in more than one place, so setting it as an option will allow your code to be less repetitive.

Edit the declaration of the defaults variable to set your defaults for the duration:

```
var defaults = {
  duration: 1000
};
```

There are two methods that you need to change. The first is the animateSlider() method. You were passing the duration and a callback into this method, but now you only need to pass in the direction and a callback. Change your animateSlider() method to look like so:

```
var animateSlider = function(direction, callback) {
  $sliderList.stop(true, true).animate({
    "margin-left" : direction + "=300px"
  }, settings.duration, callback);
};
```

Finally, edit the call to animateSlider() in the button click event handler so that you only pass in the direction, and not the duration. You could pass in a callback, but right now, you don't need to, so don't bother.

```
animateSlider((isBackButton ? "+" : "-"));
```

Next, update animateSliderToMargin:

```
var animateSliderToMargin = function(margin, callback) {
  $sliderList.stop(true, true).animate({
    "margin-left": margin
  }, settings.duration, callback);
};
```

And similarly, update the calls to it within the event handler so that they no longer pass through the duration:

```
$allButtons.on("click", function(event) {
  var isBackButton = $(this).hasClass("back");
  if(!isBackButton && isAtEnd()) {
    animateSliderToMargin(0);
  } else if(isBackButton && isAtBeginning()) {
    animateSliderToMargin(endMargin);
  } else {
    animateSlider((isBackButton ? "+" : "-"));
  }
  event.preventDefault();
});
```

You should also look out for fixed values when developing plug-ins. All of your values need to be calculated; for example, the width of each image in your slider should be calculated, not hard-coded. Although you have done that with this plug-in, there's one place we have kept a hard-coded value where it should be calculated. Can you see where?

It's in your animateSlider() method:

```
var animateSlider = function(direction, callback) {
  $sliderList.stop(true, true).animate({
    "margin-left" : direction + "=300px"
  }, settings.duration, callback);
};
```

This animates by a fixed 300 pixels every time. You should be calculating this from the width of one image. You could do this within the animateSlider() method, but you should calculate it at the very top, just after your plug-in is set up. If you did it in the animateSlider() method, it would be recalculated every single time an animation ran, which is inefficient. Add the following line just above the line that calculates the endMargin variable:

```
var imageWidth = $sliderItems.first().children("img").width();
```

You can then tidy up the endMargin variable, using that imageWidth variable that you just calculated:

```
var endMargin = -(($sliderItems.length - 1) * imageWidth);
```

And now make use of this variable in the `animateSlider()` method:

```
var animateSlider = function(direction, callback) {
  $sliderList.stop(true, true).animate({
    "margin-left" : direction + "=" + imageWidth
  }, settings.duration, callback);
};
```

You can also drop the "px" from the animation call when you pass in the width—jQuery defaults to pixels if you don't specify.

Keeping Track

Before you move on to adding keyboard support, there's one small feature we should to implement. It would be nice to display a number below the slider that correlates to the current image in the slider, so that when you first load the page, it shows 1, and when you click forward, it shows 2, and so on. Before reading to see how this can be implemented, see if you can do it yourself. You'll need to

- Have a variable to keep track of the current image.

- Update this variable every time the user goes back or forward.

- Support the infinite looping. For example, if the user is on the first image and clicks the Back button, the number shouldn't go from 1 to 0, it should go from 1 to the last image, which is 9.

- Add an element to the HTML that the number will be displayed in, and update this value every time the index changes.

Here is our solution, but attempt to do it yourself. First, create new variables:

```
var totalImages = $sliderItems.length;
var currentIndex = 1;
```

In the HTML, below the Forward link, add a quick `span` to show the value:

```
<span class="index">1</span>
```

Then add another variable just below where you assign `currentIndex` to store a reference to this new span element:

```
var $index = $(".index");
```

Add the `index` class to the same set of CSS that styles the buttons, and align the text within the span centrally. Add these styles to the bottom of your `style.css` file:

```
.button, .index {
  font-family: Arial, sans-serif;
  font-size: 14px;
  display: block;
  padding: 6px;
```

```
  border: 1px solid #ccc;
  margin: 10px 0 0 0;
}
.index {
  text-align: center;
}
```

This leaves the slider looking like Figure 11-2.

Figure 11-2. The newly styled span tag showing the index

Next, create a method called updateIndex() in your slider.jquery.js file, which takes in the new index. It then stores this in the currentIndex variable and updates the value on display within the span, using that $index variable that you created.

```
var updateIndex = function(newIndex) {
  currentIndex = newIndex;
  $index.text(currentIndex);
};
```

Finally, it's just the matter of using this method in the click event handler. The following code shows how to do this. Call it and pass in either 0 or the last number (if the slider loops from the end to the beginning).

```
$allButtons.on("click", function(event) {
  var isBackButton = $(this).hasClass("back");
  if(!isBackButton && isAtEnd()) {
    animateSliderToMargin(0);
    updateIndex(1);
  } else if(isBackButton && isAtBeginning()) {
```

```
    animateSliderToMargin(endMargin);
    updateIndex(totalImages);
  } else {
    animateSlider((isBackButton ? "+" : "-"));
  }
  event.preventDefault();
});
```

Next, you have the code that shows the new animateSlider() method. Depending on which direction the animation is going in, simply either subtract 1 from the index or add 1.

```
var animateSlider = function(direction, callback) {
  $sliderList.stop(true, true).animate({
    "margin-left" : direction + "=" + imageWidth
  }, settings.duration, callback);
  if(direction == "+") {
    // back button
    updateIndex(currentIndex - 1);
  } else {
    // forward
    updateIndex(currentIndex + 1);
  }
};
```

Of course, you can refactor that using the ternary operator. The method is now nicely trimmed down:

```
var animateSlider = function(direction, callback) {
  $sliderList.stop(true, true).animate({
    "margin-left" : direction + "=" + imageWidth
  }, settings.duration, callback);

  var increment = (direction === "+" ? -1 : 1);
  updateIndex(currentIndex + increment);
};
```

Once again, here the my entire slider.jquery.js file, so that you can easily compare your implementation of the index to ours and make sure that you're on the same page as us before you dive into adding keyboard support:

```
(function($) {
  $.fn.slider = function(options) {
    var defaults = {
      duration: 1000
    };
    var settings = $.extend({}, defaults, options);

    return this.each(function() {
      // store some initial variables
      var $slider = $(this);
      var $sliderList = $slider.children("ul");
      var $sliderItems = $sliderList.children("li");
```

```
var $allButtons = $slider.find(".button");
var $buttons = {
  forward: $allButtons.filter(".forward"),
  back: $allButtons.filter(".back")
};
var $index = $(".index");
var totalImages = $sliderItems.length;

var imageWidth = $sliderItems.first().children("img").width();
var endMargin = -(totalImages - 1) * imageWidth;

var currentIndex = 1;
var animateSlider = function(direction, callback) {
  $sliderList.stop(true, true).animate({
    "margin-left" : direction + "=" + imageWidth
  }, settings.duration, callback);

  var increment = (direction === "+" ? -1 : 1);
  updateIndex(currentIndex + increment);
};

var animateSliderToMargin = function(margin, callback) {
  $sliderList.stop(true, true).animate({
    "margin-left": margin
  }, settings.duration, callback);
};

var getLeftMargin = function() {
  return parseInt($sliderList.css("margin-left"), 10);
};

var isAtBeginning = function() {
  return getLeftMargin() === 0;
};

var isAtEnd = function() {
  return getLeftMargin() === endMargin;
};

var updateIndex = function(newIndex) {
  currentIndex = newIndex;
  $index.text(currentIndex);
};

$allButtons.on("click", function(event) {
  var isBackButton = $(this).hasClass("back");
  if(!isBackButton && isAtEnd()) {
    animateSliderToMargin(0);
    updateIndex(1);
  } else if(isBackButton && isAtBeginning()) {
    animateSliderToMargin(endMargin);
```

```
        updateIndex(totalImages);
      } else {
        animateSlider((isBackButton ? "+" : "-"));
      }
      event.preventDefault();
    });
  });
};
})(jQuery);
```

Keyboard Support

Adding keyboard support was one of the things that we purposely left out of the coverage of events in Chapters 5 and 6 so that we could cover it here. It's actually a lot simpler than you might think.

One of the events is the keyup event. This event is fired when a key is pressed and then released. All you need to do is capture that event and do something when it happens. Remember that with every event, jQuery passes through the event object; one of the properties on that event object is keyCode. It corresponds to the key that was pressed to trigger the event. Each key has a unique number, which is an integer. The two keys that you will use are the left and right arrows. The left arrow's keycode is 37, and the right arrow's is 39. If you'd like to find out keycodes for other keys, the blog article at https://www.cambiaresearch.com/articles/15/javascript-char-codes-key-codes by Cambia Research provides a comprehensive list.

You could listen for the keyup event and trigger a click event on either the Back or Forward button, depending on the keycode. To do this, you need an element to bind the keyup event to. It needs to be an element that's always in focus, so that no matter where the mouse is located when the user presses the arrows, the slider will work.

Your first thought might be to use "body", which is sensible. However, older versions of Internet Explorer are a little rough in their support for this. In our research for this book, we found that "body" didn't work on IE9 and below. It's actually best to use document.documentElement, which is a property on the document object—a DOM object that stores information about the contents of the document. documentElement contains a reference to all the contents on the page because it returns the element that is the root element—the <html> tag in browsers. Knowing this, you can bind a keyup event to it and trigger a click based on the key that was pressed:

```
$(document.documentElement).on("keyup", function(event) {
  if(event.keyCode === 37) {
    //left arrow
    $(".back").trigger("click");
  } else if (event.keyCode === 39) {
    //right arrow
    $(".forward").trigger("click");
  }
});
```

If you open your slider in the browser, you see that you can now control your slider with arrows! It's as easy as that.

Your next challenge is to automatically animate the slider every 20 seconds. To do this, you'll need to be able to animate the slider through calling a method directly, and not just through triggering a click event on the button. This is because you need to do things differently when automatically triggering an animation, compared to when the user manually clicks the button. Therefore, you're going to take the main functionality contained within the event handler and move it into its own function.

Call this function `triggerSlider()`, and take the contents of the event handler and move them into it:

```
var triggerSlider = function(direction, callback) {
  var isBackButton = (direction === "+");
  if(!isBackButton && isAtEnd()) {
    animateSliderToMargin(0, callback);
    updateIndex(1);
  } else if(isBackButton && isAtBeginning()) {
    animateSliderToMargin(endMargin, callback);
    updateIndex(totalImages);
  } else {
    animateSlider(direction, callback);
  }
};
```

This function will take one argument, the direction, which is either "+" or "-". Then set the value of `isBackButton` based on that. JavaScript will evaluate (`direction === "+"`) to either `true` or `false`, and set the result of `isBackButton` accordingly. This means your click event handler for the buttons is dramatically smaller:

```
$allButtons.on("click", function(event) {
  var isBackButton = $(this).hasClass("back");
  triggerSlider((isBackButton? "+" : "-"));
  event.preventDefault();
});
```

And you need to alter the keyup event handler to call `triggerSlider()`:

```
$(document.documentElement).on("keyup", function(event) {
  if(event.keyCode === 37) {
    triggerSlider("+");
  } else if (event.keyCode === 39) {
    triggerSlider("-");
  }
});
```

This leaves you with nicer code and a way to trigger the animation without triggering a click event. This is important, as you'll see next when you look into automatically animating your slider.

Automatic Animation

To implement automatic animation of your slider, you're going to use a JavaScript method called `setTimeout()`. It takes two arguments: a function and a time in milliseconds. The function you pass in is executed after that specific amount of time; for example:

```
setTimeout(function() { alert("hey"); }, 1000);
```

If you run this, you'll see the alert pop up, but only after 1 second. You can use this to animate your slider.

To make your slider run infinitely, you can create a function that executes and then calls setTimeout(), passing itself as the first argument. The following code demonstrates this, *but you should not execute this in a browser!* You'd get alerts infinitely.

```
var alertHey = function() {
  alert("Hey");
  setTimeout(alertHey, 1000);

}
setTimeout(alertHey, 1000);
```

The alertHey function alerts "Hey" and then runs setTimeout(), which gets called after 1 second. Once you call the function, it will continue to run every second.

Knowing this, you can implement your automatic sliding pretty easily:

```
var automaticSlide = function() {
  setTimeout(function() {
    triggerSlider("-", function() {
      automaticSlide();
    });
  }, 1000);
};
setTimeout(automaticSlide, 1000);
```

If you refresh in the browser, you should see your slider animate every second. But there's a problem! You can click, but that won't stop the animations. Navigating back is particularly difficult because the slider moves forward every second.

Before you solve this, you're going to add a new option, animationDelay, which is the period between automatic animations. Here, the default is set to 5000, which is a little higher than you had it previously. If you'd like it to be less or more, feel free to tweak to suit.

```
var defaults = {
  duration: 1000,
  animationDelay: 5000
};
```

And then update the animation code:

```
var automaticSlide = function() {
  setTimeout(function() {
    triggerSlider("-", function() {
      automaticSlide();
    });
  }, settings.animationDelay);
};
setTimeout(automaticSlide, settings.animationDelay);
```

It is possible to clear a timeout that's pending. setTimeout() returns an ID, which is the ID of the pending timeout. You can then pass this into clearTimeout() to cancel the timeout. So, you need to do the following:

- When the user clicks a button, cancel the timeout.

- Set another timeout—but for a much longer period (perhaps 30 seconds)—at which to restart the automatic animations.

- If the user clicks the button in the meantime, cancel that timeout, too.

First, insert a new line that sets the initial timeout to have its results stored in a variable, timer:

```
var timer = setTimeout(automaticSlide, settings.animationDelay);
```

Then, edit the automaticSlide() method to use that same variable:

```
var automaticSlide = function() {
  timer = setTimeout(function() {
    triggerSlider("-", function() {
      automaticSlide();
    });
  }, settings.animationDelay);
};
```

Now you have a reference to the currently set timer in the timer variable and you can cancel it by passing it through to clearTimeout(). To do this, make another utility method called resetTimer(). This should cancel the pending timeout and then set a new one, but with a much longer time period:

```
var resetTimer = function() {
  if(timer) {
    clearTimeout(timer);
  }
  timer = setTimeout(automaticSlide, 30000);
}
```

The method first checks to see if the timer variable evaluates to true, which means it contains a value. If it does, you clear the timeout. You then set up a new timeout, storing the result back to the timer variable. You then need to call this method twice: first, when the user clicks the buttons:

```
$allButtons.on("click", function(event) {
  resetTimer();
  var isBackButton = $(this).hasClass("back");
  triggerSlider((isBackButton? "+" : "-"));
  event.preventDefault();
});
```

And again when the user uses the arrow keys to navigate:

```
$(document.documentElement).on("keyup", function(event) {
  if(event.keyCode === 37) {
    resetTimer();
    triggerSlider("+");
```

```
    } else if (event.keyCode === 39) {
      resetTimer();
      triggerSlider("-");
    }
});
```

With those changes, you should be able to navigate using either the arrow keys or the buttons, without the automatic sliding getting in the way. If you wait 30 seconds, the automatic sliding should kick back in.

Bug Fixing

With any sizable plug-in like this, you're always going to have bugs crop up. We've purposely left one in to demonstrate an actual bug and show how you might solve it. Try bringing up your slider in the browser, and then rapidly pressing the left arrow button on your keyboard. If you do it enough times, you should end up with what is shown in Figure 11-3. You've managed to skip past your infinite loop detection code, and ended up on Image –9.

Figure 11-3. *Definitely a bug that needs fixing!*

Take a moment to figure out what might be happening. It's actually not very obvious at all. As a clue, the bug is in the following two methods:

```
var isAtBeginning = function() {
  return getLeftMargin() === 0;
};

var isAtEnd = function() {
  return getLeftMargin() === endMargin;
};
```

When you hit the left arrow continuously, it fires a lot of animations in a very short space of time. Although you use jQuery's stop() method to quell this, you could end up at the beginning of the slider, but with the margin not quite at 0. When a lot of animations fire quickly and then stop abruptly, you could end up at a margin that's between two images. It's then possible for the margins to not be the nice whole numbers you expect (0, 300, 600, etc.), but instead be slightly off. So you need to be less specific. If the slider is at the beginning, the left margin will be *equal to or greater than* 0. Similarly, if the slider is at the end, the left margin will be *less than or equal to* the endMargin (less than because the values are negative, remember). Go ahead and make that change:

```
var isAtBeginning = function() {
  return getLeftMargin() >= 0;
};

var isAtEnd = function() {
  return getLeftMargin() <= endMargin;
};
```

When you now run your slider and press an arrow key rapidly, you'll see it's impossible to get past the beginning or end. There is one more problem, though: it's possible for the index that's displayed to briefly be too high or low. You have images 1–9, but the index will briefly get to 0 or 10 as you hit the left arrow too quickly. Can you spot the source of this bug? It's in the animateSlider() method:

```
var animateSlider = function(direction, callback) {
  $sliderList.stop(true, true).animate({
    "margin-left" : direction + "=" + imageWidth
  }, settings.duration, callback);
  var increment = (direction === "+" ? -1 : 1);
  updateIndex(currentIndex + increment);
};
```

Here, you are updating the current index immediately after the animation is kicked off. Instead, you should be updating the current index once the animation finishes, so you should be doing it within the callback. By doing this, you ensure that once the animation is done, the index is updated as you expect. This also means the index is only updated when the animation runs through to a finish. You need to refactor your animateSlider() method, so update the index within the callback. Once you do that, you can call the callback that is passed into the animateSlider() method. This shows your refactored animateSlider() method:

```
var animateSlider = function(direction, callback) {
  $sliderList.stop(true, true).animate({
    "margin-left" : direction + "=" + imageWidth
  }, settings.duration, function() {
    var increment = (direction === "+" ? -1 : 1);
    updateIndex(currentIndex + increment);
    if(callback && typeof callback == "function") {
      callback();
    }
  });
};
```

Within the callback, you can update the index, and then call the passed in callback. Be careful here because you first need to check that the callback is set to something, and that it's a function. A quick conditional does that for you. With that, your slider is much improved and the bugs have been squished. Good work!

Summary

What a chapter! You created your very own image slider—complete with automatic animations and keyboard shortcuts—from scratch. You've made it robust and versatile by clearing animations properly and calculating all values mathematically, rather than hard-coding any of them.

So that you can admire your work, here's the full slider plug-in:

```
(function($) {

  $.fn.slider = function(options) {
    var defaults = {
      duration: 1000,
      animationDelay: 5000
    };
    var settings = $.extend({}, defaults, options);
```

```
return this.each(function() {
  // store some initial variables
  var $slider = $(this);
  var $sliderList = $slider.children("ul");
  var $sliderItems = $sliderList.children("li");
  var $allButtons = $slider.find(".button");
  var $buttons = {
    forward: $allButtons.filter(".forward"),
    back: $allButtons.filter(".back")
  };
  var $index = $(".index");
  var imageWidth = $sliderItems.first().children("img").width();
  var endMargin = -(($sliderItems.length - 1) * imageWidth);

  var totalImages = $sliderItems.length;
  var currentIndex = 1;
  var isPaused = false;

  var animateSlider = function(direction, callback) {
    $sliderList.stop(true, true).animate({
      "margin-left" : direction + "=" + imageWidth
    }, settings.duration, function() {
      var increment = (direction === "+" ? -1 : 1);
      updateIndex(currentIndex + increment);
      if(callback && typeof callback == "function") {
        callback();
      }
    });
  };

  var animateSliderToMargin = function(margin, callback) {
    $sliderList.stop(true, true).animate({
      "margin-left": margin
    }, settings.duration, callback);
  };

  var getLeftMargin = function() {
    return parseInt($sliderList.css("margin-left"), 10);
  };

  var isAtBeginning = function() {
    return getLeftMargin() >= 0;
  };

  var isAtEnd = function() {
    return getLeftMargin() <= endMargin;
  };
```

```javascript
      var updateIndex = function(newIndex) {
        currentIndex = newIndex;
        $index.text(currentIndex);
      };

      var triggerSlider = function(direction, callback) {
        var isBackButton = (direction === "+");
        if(!isBackButton && isAtEnd()) {
          animateSliderToMargin(0, callback);
          updateIndex(1);
        } else if(isBackButton && isAtBeginning()) {
          animateSliderToMargin(endMargin, callback);
          updateIndex(totalImages);
        } else {
          animateSlider(direction, callback);
        }
      };

      var automaticSlide = function() {
        timer = setTimeout(function() {
          triggerSlider("-", function() {
            automaticSlide();
          });
        }, settings.animationDelay);
      };
      var timer = setTimeout(automaticSlide, settings.animationDelay);
      var resetTimer = function() {
        if(timer) {
          clearTimeout(timer);
        }
        timer = setTimeout(automaticSlide, 30000);
      }

      $allButtons.on("click", function(event) {
        resetTimer();
        var isBackButton = $(this).hasClass("back");
        triggerSlider((isBackButton? "+" : "-"));
        event.preventDefault();
      });

      $(document.documentElement).on("keyup", function(event) {
        if(event.keyCode === 37) {
          resetTimer();
          triggerSlider("+");
        } else if (event.keyCode === 39) {
          resetTimer();
          triggerSlider("-");
        }
      });
    });
  }
})(jQuery);
```

All the code for this chapter and all the others is available to download from the Apress web site.

Conclusion

That brings us to the end of the book. We hope that you finish reading it feeling confident that you can utilize JavaScript and jQuery to solve any relevant problem that you face. In addition to demonstrating practical uses, we tried to demonstrate important concepts and approaches that will hopefully enable you to tackle problems and produce a robust solution. If you're wondering where to go from here, we recommend sticking with the jQuery skills you've learned from this book, and if you'd like to dive further into JavaScript, we'd advise reading a book on pure JavaScript. jQuery is just JavaScript, and the better you are at JavaScript, the better you are at jQuery.

Index

Get the eBook for only $5!

Why limit yourself?

With most of our titles available in both PDF and ePUB format, you can access your content wherever and however you wish—on your PC, phone, tablet, or reader.

Since you've purchased this print book, we are happy to offer you the eBook for just $5.

To learn more, go to http://www.apress.com/companion or contact support@apress.com.

Apress®

Printed in the United States
By Bookmasters